UNIDIR/2000/20

Tactical Nuclear Weapons

Options for Control

William C. POTTER, Nikolai SOKOV,
Harald MÜLLER and Annette SCHAPER

UNIDIR
United Nations Institute for Disarmament Research
Geneva, Switzerland

NOTE

The designations employed and the presentation of the material in this publication do not imply the expression of any opinion whatsoever on the part of the Secretariat of the United Nations concerning the legal status of any country, territory, city or area, or of its authorities, or concerning the delimitation of its frontiers or boundaries.

*
* *

The views expressed in this paper are those of the authors and do not necessarily reflect the views of the United Nations Secretariat.

UNIDIR/2000/20

UNITED NATIONS PUBLICATION

Sales No. GV.E.00.0.21

ISBN 92-9045-136-X

CONTENTS

Page

Acronyms v
Preface vii

Part I
The Nature of the Problem
William C. Potter and Nikolai Sokov
Center for Non-proliferation Studies,
Monterey Institute of International Studies 1

Properties of Tactical Nuclear Weapons 4
Deterioration of United States-Russian Relations 4
The Demise of Negotiating Arms Control Accords 5
Recent Developments in Military Doctrines 6
The 1991-1992 United States-Soviet Initiatives:
    Strengths and Weaknesses 8
Approaches to Strengthening the 1991-1992 Regime:
    Lessons from Theory 10
A Preliminary List of Steps Towards the Control and/or
    Elimination of TNWs 12
Transparency Measures 13
Freeze on Deployments 13
Formalization of the 1991 Unilateral Declarations 14
Additional Unilateral Initiatives 14
Formal and Informal Nuclear-Weapon-Free Zones (NWFZs) . 15
Treatment of TNWs as a Separate Issue 15
Utilization of the NPT Review Process 15
Multilateral Agreements on TNWs 16
Priority Measures 16
Conclusion 18

Part II
Definitions, Types, Missions, Risks and Options for Control: A European Perspective
Harald Müller and Annette Schaper
Peace Research Institute Frankfurt, Germany   19

Introduction 21
"Tactical" and "Strategic" in Classical Military Thought 22
TNWs in Historical Perspective 23
Current Status of TNWs 26
Does the Definition of TNWs on the Basis of Range
    Make Sense? 31
Variations of Definitions for TNWs 33
Is a Definition Needed? 34
TNWs in Present NATO Doctrine 36
Risks Inherent in TNWs 38
Conclusion 41
What Can be Done to Address the Problem? 42
Final Comments 49

Appendix 51

Recent UNIDIR Publications   79

ACRONYMS

AAA	Air-to-air missile
ABM	Anti-ballistic missile
ACM	Advanced cruise missile
ADM	Atomic demolition munition
AFAP	Artillery-fired atomic projectile
ALCM	Air-launched cruise missile
ASM	Air-to-surface missile
ASW	Anti-submarine warfare
CDI	Center for Defense Information
CEP	Circular error probable
CFE	Conventional Forces in Europe (Treaty)
CIA	Central Intelligence Agency (United States)
CTBT	Comprehensive Test Ban Treaty
DPRK	Democratic People's Republic of Korea
FAS	Federation of American Scientists
GLCM	Ground-launched cruise missile
HWT	Heavy weight torpedoes
IAEA	International Atomic Energy Agency
ICBM	Intercontinental ballistic missile
INF	Intermediate-Range Nuclear Forces (Treaty)
MRS	Multiple-rocket system
NATO	North Atlantic Treaty Organization
NMD	National Missile Defense
NNWS	Non-nuclear weapon State
NPT	Non-Proliferation Treaty
NRDC	Natural Resources Defence Council
NWFZ	Nuclear Weapon-Free Zone
NWS	Nuclear Weapon State
PALs	Permissive action links
PRC	People's Republic of China
PJC	Permanent Joint Council (NATO-Russia)
PrepCom	Preparatory Commission
SALT	Strategic Arms Limitation Treaty
SLBM	Submarine-launched ballistic missile
SLCM	Sea-launched cruise missile

SRAM	Short-range attack missile
SRBM	Short-range ballistic missile
START	Strategic Arms Reduction Treaty
TEL	Transporter erector launcher
TNW	Tactical nuclear weapon
USAF	United States Air Force
WMD	Weapons of mass destruction

PREFACE

It is hard to believe that a decade after the Bush-Gorbachov unilateral declarations on tactical nuclear weapons this class of weapons would once again be a cause for concern.

At the end of the Cold War, it was well understood that tactical nuclear weapons, which were forward-based and integrated with conventional forces, were a particularly dangerous category of nuclear weapons. The United States decided to eliminate all its ground-based tactical nuclear weapons and remove all nuclear weapons from surface ships and attack submarines. Russia had already withdrawn its tactical nuclear weapons from all but three Soviet republics and further reciprocated in kind. However, there was never any formal agreement on the removal and elimination of tactical nuclear weapons. Despite periodic updates on progress, data were never agreed, only proportions of numbers to be eliminated or stored were declared. There is still today a great deal of uncertainty over the implementation of the 1991 unilateral declarations.

Since 1999, the spectre of tactical nuclear weapons has again been raised as a serious concern. The culminated response by Russia to NATO enlargement, the conflict over Kosovo, and United States proposals to modify the Anti-Ballistic Missile Treaty, thus allowing national missile defences, has led to renewed interest in tactical nuclear weapons in Russia and to calls to remanufacture or modernize the existing tactical nuclear force within the near future. In addition, regional nuclear weapons developments, particularly in South Asia following the nuclear weapons tests by India and Pakistan in 1998, have fostered concerns over the deployment of tactical nuclear weapons in Asia and the Middle East.

In response to these developments, and with the support of the United Nations Secretary General's Advisory Board on Disarmament Matters, UNIDIR began a study on the situation regarding tactical nuclear weapons. In March 2000, UNIDIR hosted a workshop in Geneva at which papers analysing such issues as the current situation, numbers and definitions, and regional approaches were presented.

The discussion at the meeting highlighted a number of points. It is clear, particularly when considering the possession of nuclear weapons by States other than the *de jure* nuclear weapon states, that the definitions of tactical nuclear weapons are inadequate. If strategic nuclear weapons are defined in terms of the capability and mission to hit the heart of an adversary's homeland, then the range of these weapons is not always the key factor in their definition, neither is the explosive yield. In the United States-Russia dialogue on such weapons however, geographical range has been the overriding feature in attempts to delineate tactical from strategic. A number of participants argued that the subdivision of nuclear weapons into strategic and tactical was not as useful as treating all nuclear weapons collectively. Others felt strongly that the particular dangers of tactical nuclear weapons, with regard to their missions, command and control, were sufficient to warrant their separate and urgent treatment.

The March meeting also debated the role of tactical nuclear weapons beyond the national boundaries of the possessor States, focusing much attention on tactical nuclear weapons in NATO Europe and on NATO doctrine. The large numerical superiority of Russian deployed tactical nuclear weapons and recent changes in Russian nuclear weapons doctrine was cause for increasing concern. A number of approaches to dealing with the tactical nuclear weapons issue were put forward and are outlined in this book by the authors. It is hoped that these prposals will continue to be

I would particularly like to thank the authors of the papers: Harald Müller and Annette Schaper of the Peace Research Institute Frankfurt, Germany, and William C. Potter and Nikolai Sokov of the Center for Nonproliferation Studies, Monterey Institute of International Studies, USA. Thanks also go to Tariq Rauf of the Center for Nonproliferation Studies, Monterey Institute of International Studies, USA, and Hazel Tamano and Jackie Seck of UNIDIR for their contributions to the project. Gratitude also to the generosity of the funders of the project: The Ford Foundation, the Governments of Canada, Italy, Finland, the Netherlands, Norway and the United Kingdom.

Patricia Lewis
Director, UNIDIR

PART I

The Nature of the Problem[*]

**William C. Potter
and
Nikolai Sokov**

**Center for Non-proliferation Studies,
Monterey Institute of International Studies**

---

[*] Report initially prepared for a discussion session on tactical nuclear weapons organized by the United Nations Institute for Disarmament Research (UNIDIR), Geneva, 21-22 March 2000. The authors thank UNIDIR as well as countries and foundations which have contributed funds to this timely project. Nikolai Sokov expresses special gratitude to the Ploughshares Fund that supported his research on the topic.

Tactical nuclear weapons (TNWs) are the category of American and Russian nuclear arsenals which is the least regulated by arms control agreements. They are only subject to an informal regime created by unilateral, parallel declarations made by George Bush and Mikhail Gorbachov in the autumn of 1991, the latter of which was subsequently affirmed and expanded upon by Boris Yeltsin in January 1992. Since then, TNWs have not figured prominently in the bilateral United States-Russian arms control and disarmament agenda.

This lack of attention to TNWs is unfortunate and dangerous given their large number, the risks of early and/or unauthorized use, and their vulnerability to theft. The regime itself is increasingly precarious since it is not legally binding, does not provide for data exchanges, and lacks a verification mechanism. As such, it is poorly equipped to withstand increasing challenges, such as the deterioration in United States-Russian political relations; the growing scepticism in both countries about the role of arms control treaties in providing for their national security; the revival of interest in TNWs in both Russia and, to a lesser extent, in the United States; growing pressure in Russia to re-manufacture and/or modernize its TNW force as the existing stocks near the end of their service life; and finally, the renewed interest in TNWs in South Asia following the nuclear detonations by India and Pakistan in 1998.

Although the United States-Russian 1991-1992 unilateral statements have resulted in significant reductions in TNWs, the future viability of the regime is at risk. This chapter examines:

- The nature of the problem, which relates to the properties of TNWs, the dynamic of the United States-Russian relationship, and developments in American and Russian military doctrines;
- The shortcomings of the 1991-1992 informal regime and alternative approaches for rectifying them;
- Concrete policy recommendations for both the immediate and longer term.

Properties of Tactical Nuclear Weapons

The dangers associated with TNWs relate to both their physical properties and the policies for their deployment and employment. The small size of the weapons and the absence among older generations of electronic locks or permissive action links (PALs) contribute to their vulnerability to theft and unauthorized use. The modes of their basing and of their prescribed use also pose major problems in terms of their physical and political control. These risks derive from several factors:

1. The intended use of TNWs in battlefield and theatre-level operations in conjunction with conventional forces encourages their forward basing, especially in times of crisis, and in certain situations movement of TNWs might actually provoke a pre-emptive strike by the other side instead of deterring it; and

2. An orientation towards the employment of TNWs in conjunction with conventional forces and a concern about their survivability argues for the pre-delegation of launch authority to lower level commanders in the theatre, especially once hostilities commence. This might result in diminished control by the political leadership over TNWs.

Thus, the very existence of TNWs in national arsenals increases the risk of proliferation and reduces the nuclear threshold, making the nuclear balance less stable. If the two leading nuclear Powers appear to consider TNWs essential and usable, others may well emulate this example.

Deterioration of United States-Russian Relations

The deterioration in United States-Russian relations is evident in many forums, including the arms control arena. This erosion impacts upon the issue of TNWs in several ways. First, it has slowed progress towards conclusion of a Strategic Arms Reduction Treaty (START) III. This stalemate in strategic arms control, which was only broken in April 2000 with the Dumas ratification of START II, directly relates to TNWs since both sides have avoided separate negotiations on this issue. According to the joint statement adopted by Bill Clinton and Boris Yeltsin in April 1997, TNWs were to be discussed in the context of START III, although this objective no longer appears to be certain.

The cooling of United States-Russian relations, especially following the North Atlantic Treaty Organization (NATO) military campaign in former Yugoslavia, has also reduced the already limited transparency with respect to TNWs. Although the 1991 parallel declarations did not provide for data exchange regarding implementation of the initiatives, information had been exchanged at meetings of the NATO-Russia Permanent Joint Council (PJC). The breakdown of that mechanism following the actions in former Yugoslavia have precluded data exchanges at that venue, at least temporarily.

THE DEMISE OF NEGOTIATING ARMS CONTROL ACCORDS

There are disturbing signals from both Washington and Moscow that many policy makers have begun to question the efficacy of arms control treaties in combating the spread of weapons of mass destruction (WMD) and in providing for United States and Russian national security. This tendency is apparent in the defeat last year in the United States Senate of the Comprehensive Test Ban Treaty (CTBT), the extended delay by Russia in ratifying START II, and the sentiment among many in the United States Congress that the United States must proceed with a system of National Missile Defense (NMD) with or without Russian consent to modification of the Anti-Ballistic Missile (ABM) Treaty. Should that NMD scenario unfold, there is a very good prospect that Russia will respond by withdrawing not only from START I and START II, but also possibly from the 1991-1992 parallel, unilateral declarations.

This threat is not new. Since the fall of 1996, a number of Russian officials have warned that NATO enlargement and, later, military action in Kosovo might necessitate the scrapping of the 1991 declarations and the redeployment of TNWs in Belarus, the Kaliningrad oblast, and on naval ships in the Baltic Sea. A decision by the United States to abrogate the ABM Treaty, however, would probably precipitate another kind of NMD, what George Bunn has called: No More Disarmament. Such a policy would be in keeping with the more general questioning by current Russian policy makers of the efficacy of the arms control legacy of the 1970s, 1980s, and early 1990s and its relevance to Russian security interests in the new millennium. This rethinking may be hinted at in the 2000 National Security Concept that not only emphasizes the importance of nuclear weapons, but also suggests that Russia should adapt the existing arms control and disarmament agreements to the new conditions in international relations...[1]

RECENT DEVELOPMENTS IN MILITARY DOCTRINES

A number of factors contribute to the renewed interest in TNWs in Russia and the United States. In the more optimistic scenario, in which deep reductions of strategic weapons are accomplished for example, a START III environment in which strategic weapons are reduced to the level of 1,500-2,000, the share of TNWs in the nuclear arsenals of the two countries will increase substantially. This will likely increase their share of assigned nuclear missions.

In Russia, regardless of progress on the START front, TNWs also acquired greater significance because of the deterioration of Russia's conventional forces and its growing reliance on nuclear arms as a poor man's counter to the revolution in military affairs and the technological breakthrough by the United States in costly, advanced conventional arms. Indeed, while chemical weapons are often said to be a poor man's nuclear weapon, for Russia, nuclear weapons are a poor man's substitute for advanced conventional arms. Regrettably, but understandably, in Russia nuclear weapons in general and TNWs in particular are enjoying a renaissance.

This trend was observable as early as 1996 when some Russian officials began to threaten withdrawal from the 1991 TNW regime in

---

[1] National Security Concept of the Russian Federation. Approved by the Decree of the President of the Russian Federation No. 1300 of 17 December 1997, version of the Decree of the President of the Russian Federation No. 24 of 10 January 2000.

response to NATO's planned enlargement. Although those initial threats represented primarily an emotional response, the debate over NATO enlargement stimulated interest in Russia in TNWs as a counterweight to NATO conventional forces, an interest that has not diminished.

In 1999 Russia launched a fundamental reassessment of its military doctrine, a process stimulated to a large extent by the war in former Yugoslavia. Tactical nuclear weapons figure prominently in the ongoing debate. Current Russian thinking on TNWs is informed, to a large degree, by American concepts developed during the Cold War, which have been adapted to the specific circumstances Russia faces, and is likely to face, in future conflicts. For NATO, TNWs were an instrument for deterring a large-scale attack; for Russia TNWs are supposed to help de-escalate a limited conflict, compensating not only for numbers, but also and probably chiefly for the superior quality of NATO/American conventional weapons. The broadened scope of missions for nuclear weapons in Russia is referred to under the name of expanded deterrence. This innovation is reflected in the increased integration of nuclear weapons into war planning, and was evident in the West 99 military exercises.

One can also observe a shift in Russian diplomacy, which now interprets the Tashkent Treaty on Collective Security to allow for Russian deployment of nuclear weapons in Central Asia under certain conditions. This policy shift, evident after April 1999, is apparent in quiet but effective Russian diplomacy to weaken the Central Asian Nuclear-Weapons-Free Zone Treaty that is currently under negotiation.

For its part, the United States continues to maintain a small stock of TNWs in Europe. These weapons, of dubious military value, are regarded in Washington as still useful for the political purpose of signalling a United States commitment to its European allies. TNWs are also promoted by some in Washington as a useful deterrent against possible chemical and biological threats from rogue States.

It is interesting and important to note that revival of interest in tactical nuclear weapons in Russia and, to a lesser extent, in the United States is not correlated with the dynamic of changes in their quantity. TNW arsenals are dwindling in at least four out of the five original nuclear-weapon States. The danger to the 1991-1992 regime stems from qualitative developments, including doctrinal changes, deployment of TNWs in the manner inconsistent with the regime, as well as new types and modifications of TNWs. It also relates to the weakness of the regime, which is a function of the manner in which it was created.

THE 1991-1992 UNITED STATES-SOVIET INITIATIVES: STRENGTHS AND WEAKNESSES

On 17 September 1991, George Bush announced that the United States would eliminate its entire worldwide inventory of ground-launched TNWs, and would remove all nuclear weapons from surface ships and attack submarines. This initiative, following the failed coup attempt on 19-21 August, was prompted by the mounting concern about the security of nuclear weapons in the Soviet Union. It was designed to prompt a reciprocal response, which would facilitate the process of TNW consolidation and reduction.

One reason for the choice of a unilateral statement instead of a negotiated treaty was indicated in the statement itself: events demanded swifter, bolder action than long-drawn negotiations could afford. It also was easier to enlist the support of the United States armed forces for a non-binding initiative than for one that required a verification regime, especially one which, by virtue of the weapons at issue, would have to be more intrusive than any prior accord.

Mikhail Gorbachov responded promptly and positively to the Bush initiative on 5 October, largely reciprocating in kind, with relatively few minor modifications. The Soviet Government saw it as an opportunity to achieve its long-standing objective of reducing United States tactical nuclear weapons in Europe. Consolidation was much less of a concern because by that time tactical nuclear weapons had been withdrawn from all Soviet republics except those where strategic weapons were also deployed (i.e. Belarus, Ukraine, and Kazakhstan). The Soviet military had initiated this withdrawal in early 1990, and none too soon: in at least one case, in Azerbaijan, there was an attempt by the local Popular Front to prevent their withdrawal.

Having recognized Western concerns in the aftermath of the aborted August coup, relevant agencies of the Soviet Government began preparations for formal negotiations on TNW disarmament, and by the time of the Bush initiative the work was in full swing. Although the disarmament method chosen by the Americans was accepted, there was also hope among some government players in Moscow that formal talks would commence as well, and their failure to do so provoked some dissatisfaction. Nevertheless, in early 1992, President Yeltsin affirmed, with minor additions, Russia's adherence to implementation of Gorbachov's declaration.

These parallel declarations provide for removal to central storage facilities or elimination of all tactical nuclear warheads except for a limited number of gravity bombs which remain deployed (i.e. usable at short notice). Also included were systems whose precise classification was contested: long-range nuclear sea-launched cruise missiles (SLCMs). Reductions (both central storage and elimination) measured in thousands of warheads represent the single largest reduction of nuclear warheads, surpassing all other agreements between the United States and the Soviet Union/Russia. The target date for implementation is the year 2000, and the reductions may well be completed on time.

The lack of a formal treaty, however, resulted in the absence of any kind of hard data on the existing stockpiles as well as on the number of warheads to be put in central storage, eliminated, or deployed. The initiatives only contained the *share* of warheads subject to elimination, and inevitably produced two unwelcome consequences which haunt the United States-Russian and international arms control agenda today: uncertainty with respect to their implementation and considerable disparity of numbers.

Periodically, both countries have updated each other and other countries on the status of reductions. This process became more formal in 1997 when the NATO-Russia PJC emerged as a venue for exchanges of information with respect to TNW reductions. Still, even in that forum, the sides only discussed the share of warheads eliminated or transferred to central storage, but not absolute numbers. In 1999, in the wake of the NATO bombing of former Yugoslavia, contacts in the PJC were severely limited and information exchanges on TNWs stopped. One can only hope that they will resume now that there is an understanding that the PJC will resume its work.

APPROACHES TO STRENGTHENING THE 1991-1992 REGIME: LESSONS FROM THEORY

A fundamental property of international security regimes is the provision of predictability which mitigates the impact of anarchy in inter-State relations and weakens the propensity to plan policies proceeding from worst-case scenarios. Not only are States interested in obtaining accurate information about other States, but they also seek to provide similar information about themselves to dispel the fears of others.

International security regimes, including arms control agreements, facilitate this process. By entering into agreements, States send a clear signal about their preferences and intentions. They also constrain future policy choices because withdrawal from the agreement can have legal, political, material, and other costs. Limits on the numbers, types, deployment patterns, and modernization of weapons help to reduce the risk that the other side can gain unilateral advantage. Verification procedures enhance the acquisition of reliable evidence that the other side is not acting contrary to the accord or preparing to withdraw secretly from the agreement.

Regimes vary widely in their scope and legal nature and, consequently, the predictability they provide. Although the value of the existing TNW regime is undeniable, it is deficient on many counts. An analysis of these deficiencies suggests a number of options for improving the regime.

The existing TNW regime:

1. Is not legally binding, and each side can withdraw from its obligations without any notification. The absence of limitations on and/or prior notification about withdrawal can breed suspicion and planning on worst-case scenarios;

2. It provides for minimal information exchange, which in turn contributes to a high level of uncertainty. Uncertainty is generated by:

    - The absence of baseline information about the stockpiles at the moment of regime inception; consequently the obligations with respect to the reduction of a certain *share* of the original arsenal have limited utility;
    - In the absence of verification mechanisms, it is impossible to ascertain that the declared reductions are being implemented;
    - Exchange of information about progress in reductions is conducted on a case-by-case basis, outside a formal framework;

3. It does not limit research and development of new types of nuclear weapons, or the modification of old ones, and does not restrict the production of warheads whether existing or new types;

4. Its low institutionalization inhibits amendments or its replacement by a new regime. In effect, any revision is also a violation. For example, if Russia chose to change the mixture of weapons without increasing their number or even in the context of deeper reductions (i.e. deploy land-based missiles at the expense of gravity bombs) the regime might collapse, despite the wishes of both sides;

5. It is highly vulnerable to proposed revisions of the ABM Treaty and to the overall reassessment by Russia of the arms control commitments undertaken previously by the Kremlin. Russia is in a process of redefining its national interests, and may decide to revisit other agreements, including the Intermediate-Range Nuclear Forces (INF) Treaty, START I and II, as well as its 1991-1992 obligations with respect to tactical nuclear weapons if the ABM Treaty is abrogated or substantially modified;

6. The absence of limitations on the deployment of TNWs creates a further strain on East-West security relations. The capability to pre-deploy TNWs in case of conflict creates uncertainty about the intent of the other side and raises the fear of early use of nuclear weapons.

This assessment of the informal TNW regime provides a useful lesson about the inherent limitations of unilateral and/or parallel actions as a method of disarmament. In the last several years, this method has become popular among proponents of disarmament, probably in response to the stalled START II ratification in Russia and disillusionment with the overall progress of United States-Russian nuclear arms reductions. Enthusiasm about unilateral actions, however, is as much a sign of desperation as optimism. In fact, opponents of disarmament also promote unilateralism and claim that treaties are not really necessary. One can imagine how the ongoing debate about the ABM Treaty would look if the Treaty were instead an informal regime consisting of unilateral statements by Brezhnev and Nixon.

To be sure, unilateral parallel measures may facilitate disarmament by circumventing lengthy formal negotiations and even more difficult ratification processes. They allow countries to implement quickly measures that they are ready to undertake anyway and only need they a sign from the other side that their initiative will be reciprocated. At the same time, they overlook the most basic properties of international regimes, which guarantee stability and insure against withdrawal.

Unilateral measures only make sense if they are complemented subsequently by formal negotiations, which lead to legally binding agreements replete with verification provisions. In this respect, 1991 and 1992 represent not only the years of achievement on TNW disarmament, but also a period of a missed opportunity: a unique time when the United States was *already* and Russia was *still* in favour of TNW reductions. In short, unilateral measures are most effective as a precursor to formal treaties, not as their substitute.

A Preliminary List of Steps Towards the Control and/or Elimination of TNWs

If the bad news is that the informal United States-Russian TNW regime is at risk, the good news is that the long-neglected issue finally has begun to receive more attention. This development was most apparent at the May 1999 NPT Preparatory Commission (PrepCom) meeting where a surprisingly large and diverse group of States spoke out about the compelling need to address TNW disarmament immediately. Among the more forceful proponents of this view were Canada, Finland, Iran, Nigeria, and Switzerland. Although Russia objected to language proposed by the chairman of the PrepCom in his Working Paper of 20 May to reaffirm the need for the nuclear-weapon States to reduce further their reliance on non-strategic nuclear weapons and to pursue negotiations on their elimination as an integral part of their overall nuclear disarmament activities, the chair of the Russian delegation did take positive note, in his opening statement in the general debate, of Russia's full and consistent implementation of the declared TNW initiatives made by President Gorbachov and reaffirmed by President Yeltsin.

There are no easy, practical solutions to the problems of TNW arms control and disarmament. A preliminary and partial list of measures that may merit serious consideration, however, is presented below. No attempt is made to address the political, economic, bureaucratic, and verification merits and liabilities of these approaches. Following this list, a set of priority measures aimed at strengthening the 1991-1992 regime is provided.

Transparency Measures

There are no official, public data on the number or location of deployed or non-deployed warheads for TNWs. There is a similar data deficiency with respect to the number of eliminated nuclear charges. A potentially important next step in controlling and/or reducing further TNWs is for the nuclear-weapon States to exchange data on the number of their current TNW stocks by category (i.e. deployed, reserve/long-term storage, slated for elimination). It would also be useful to exchange data on the pace of TNW reductions since 1991 and the distribution of remaining TNWs by region.

Freeze on Deployments

Another possible option is the negotiation of a freeze on both the number and location of TNW deployments. Such a freeze could apply initially to the area covered by the Conventional Forces in Europe (CFE) Treaty from the Atlantic to the Urals. A freeze that contained a provision for reciprocal on-site inspections could provide the basis for the reduction in, and eventually the elimination of, TNWs in the region covered by the freeze.

FORMALIZATION OF THE 1991 UNILATERAL DECLARATIONS

Although the 1991 unilateral declarations appear to have been implemented, they can be reversed at any time. It therefore may be desirable to codify the existing declarations into a legally binding treaty, ideally with verification provisions. Such an approach has been advocated by Norwegian and Swedish officials since 1996, but with little additional international support to date. At the initial stage, formalization of the informal 1991-1992 TNW regime only would require conversion of the existing texts of the relevant unilateral statements into legally binding language. Data exchange on TNWs could also be included. At a later stage, the more difficult task of negotiating verification measures and deeper reductions could be undertaken.

A variant of this proposal, which might be more attractive to Moscow, would be to revise partially the coverage of the 1991 regime in a codified, legally binding version. More specifically, Russia probably would prefer the option to deploy a limited number of land-based or sea-based TNWs at the expense of air-based TNWs.

ADDITIONAL UNILATERAL INITIATIVES

The argument can be made that the dissolution of the Warsaw Pact has removed whatever security rationale there was for the deployment of TNWs in Europe. The political justification for retaining TNWs in Europe also may be outdated. If so, it may be desirable for the United States to declare its intention unilaterally to return to United States territory all of its air-based TNWs currently deployed in Europe. This pronouncement, which would lead to the elimination of all United States TNWs in Europe, could go a long way towards dispelling Russian fears about NATO and could help to revive the spirit of the parallel 1991 initiatives.

FORMAL AND INFORMAL NUCLEAR-WEAPON-FREE ZONES (NWFZs)

There is a long history of proposals to create a NWFZ in Central and Eastern Europe. Although the logic of a NWFZ in the region may continue to make sense, the political prospects for such a formal arrangement appear to be slim in the foreseeable future. The gradual emergence of a de facto NWFZ in much of Europe, however, could develop if new NATO parties emulated the Norwegian or Spanish precedents regarding non-deployment. Also potentially significant as a TNW disarmament measure is the creation of a NWFZ in Central Asia; development that has gained considerable momentum since February 1997 and has produced a draft treaty that is nearly complete.

TREATMENT OF TNWs AS A SEPARATE ISSUE

The nuclear-weapon States have shown little inclination to jump-start TNW negotiations, and the START process remains the designated negotiating forum for TNWs. Given the delayed beginning of START III and the complexities associated with its negotiation, it may be desirable to initiate separate negotiations on TNWs.

UTILIZATION OF THE NPT REVIEW PROCESS[2]

Very little attention was given at the 1997 PrepCom to the issue of TNWs. A number of States parties, however, did address the topic in the

---

[2] In May 2000, a month after the UNIDIR workshop, the 2000 NPT Review Conference included a plank on TNWs in its final document. The Nuclear Disarmament Plan of Action stipulates that nuclear-weapon States would take steps, in a way that promotes international stability and based on the principle of undiminished security for all, towards the further reduction of non-strategic nuclear weapons, based on unilateral initiatives and as an integral part of the nuclear arms reduction and disarmament process. This reference is the first time an NPT Review Conference has agreed upon language regarding TNW disarmament.

1998 session and considerable interest in the issue was apparent at the 1999 session. A carefully conceived initiative by influential States parties at the 2000 NPT Review Conference regarding selected TNW disarmament approaches such as the adoption of transparency measures could build significant international support for timely TNW disarmament action. It may also be opportune for States parties to consider inclusion of language calling for progress on TNW disarmament as a specific objective for a revised set of Principles and Objectives for Nuclear Non-Proliferation and Disarmament or for a forward-looking document of another name.

MULTILATERAL AGREEMENTS ON TNWS

An important long-term objective, which will be difficult to achieve, is an international and universally applicable treaty on TNWs, which would ban nuclear weapons of certain agreed categories. A potentially controversial aspect of a multilateral agreement on TNWs is the definition of the systems covered by the treaty, since delivery systems defined as TNWs in the bilateral United States-Russian context may be viewed as strategic by otner States. As a consequence, it may be necessary to adopt a different definition for a multilateral TNW accord.

PRIORITY MEASURES

As noted earlier, there are both general dangers associated with the properties of TNWs and specific challenges to the 1991-1992 parallel, unilateral declarations. This informal regime, one of the most significant arms control and disarmament accomplishments of the 1990s, is particularly vulnerable to the impact of both new Russian thinking about nuclear weapons and possible United States withdrawal from the ABM Treaty. A high priority should be given to reinforcing the regime and erecting a fire wall to prevent its erosion and collapse.

Among the most important steps that should be taken are (1) the reaffirmation by the United States and Russia in a joint statement of their continued commitment to the 1991 parallel, unilateral statements, or (2) preferably the signing of an executive agreement to that effect. Ideally, action of this sort should be taken at an early Clinton-Putin summit meeting, before Russia commits to new TNW production or deployments. It could, but would not necessarily need to, be part of a larger deal involving the issues of ABM Treaty modification and START III.

It would also be highly desirable, although much more difficult politically, to codify the existing declarations into a legally binding treaty, preferably with data exchange and verification provisions. Concerted efforts should be made to reach an early agreement on the initiation of negotiations on TNW reductions. Although these negotiations could conceivably be held within the START III framework, this forum is already burdened by other issues and it would probably be desirable to address TNWs in a separate, dedicated negotiation.

The two Presidents could start by converting the existing texts of the relevant unilateral statements into a legally binding executive agreement and exchange at least basic data. They could also agree to begin negotiations on verification measures and/or deeper reductions. Although verification of a TNW regime would be extremely complex, it should not be insurmountable and would be facilitated by the procedures already in place for the START, INF, and CFE treaties.

The goal of securing effective verification provisions should be especially attractive to the United States, which to date has had little success in promoting transparency with respect to Russian TNWs. Russia, for its part, is likely to be wary of increased transparency, but under certain circumstances might be receptive to a legally binding accord because of the greater predictability it would afford. Of special interest to Moscow in this regard are the limitations on sea-launched cruise missiles and the preclusion of rapid United States redeployments of TNWs in Europe. These concerns were reportedly among the factors behind a bold proposal restricting sub-strategic nuclear forces that was prepared in the late summer of 1991 by the Russian Foreign Ministry and endorsed by the General Staff, but was pre-empted by President Bush's September 1991 unilateral declaration.

One can identify logical reasons why Russia should be interested in codifying the 1991 initiatives. Nevertheless, Russian concerns about a United States/NATO advantage in conventional (and especially advanced conventional) forces, as well as fears in Moscow about further NATO enlargement and preparations by the United States for possible deployment of a National Missile Defense system, mean that the impetus for strengthening the informal TNW regime will have to come from the United States. This initiative should be supported strongly by European allies of the United States who have the most to gain by reinforcing the existing regime and who should welcome, rather than fear, the consequences of greater transparency with respect to TNWs.

Conclusion

One should not underestimate the difficulty of implementing any of the aforementioned proposals. Recent international developments, however, clearly demonstrate that the overall situation with respect to TNWs is serious and requires urgent and concerted action. We cannot wait for START III. Nor should we assume that a future START III Treaty will, in fact, cover TNWs simply because the March 1997 Helsinki Joint Statement allowed for the exploration, in the context of that treaty, of measures related to TNWs. Finally, even if one is successful in moving forward on TNW disarmament in the bilateral United States-Russian context, this progress is only the first, albeit a critical step on a longer road towards global elimination of this class of nuclear weapons.

Given the renewed interest in TNWs in Russia, and to a lesser extent in the United States, other States will have to take an active role in devising and promoting TNW arms control and disarmament. To do so will require considerable political courage, creativity and perseverance. To keep silent and to ignore the issue, however, is to accept the probability of the unravelling of one of the most successful disarmament accomplishments and the emergence of a new tactical nuclear arms race.

PART II

Definitions, Types, Missions, Risks and Options for Control:

A European Perspective

**Harald Müller
and
Annette Schaper**

Peace Research Institute Frankfurt, Germany

INTRODUCTION

This chapter inquires into the definitional and other conceptual aspects of tactical nuclear weapons (TNWs). It uses historical examples drawn mainly from the evolution of North Atlantic Treaty Organization (NATO) doctrine and hardware to illustrate the problems that the notion of "tactical" poses in the nuclear age. We conclude that a satisfactory, universally valid definition of TNWs does not exist. While "tactical" depicts military factors that are meant to affect a battle, weapons as such cannot be classified as tactical or otherwise on the basis of their inherent technical properties alone. "Tactical", thus, is a contextually dependent attribute whose ascription to different weapon systems varies with the geo-strategic environment in which these are deployed.

So-called TNWs emerged early in the nuclear age. They acquired a particular political and military importance in the context of the European security situation and the inner workings of the Atlantic Alliance during and after the Cold War. With the exception of those weapon systems involved in the Intermediate-Range Nuclear Forces (INF) Treaty of 1987, they were never subject to arms control or disarmament regulations. The other major achievement, the unilateral pledges issued by Presidents Bush and Gorbachov in 1991 to redeploy and reduce this category of weapons, was never codified. As the strategic situation has so vastly changed since, and as TNWs present specific risks, the time has come to take a fresh look at possibilities for their control, not least from a European perspective.

This chapter addresses three key aspects of TNWs: definitions, types and missions, and risks and options for control. The discussion begins with a look at the meanings of "tactical" and "strategic" in classical military thought and the modification of these meanings with the advent of air war theory in the inter-war period and in the evolution of nuclear doctrine in the course of the Cold War. It then goes on to show the relativity of the prevailing definitional criterion of TNWs—range—in terms of different regional geo-strategic contexts, and to critically explore a variety of other alternative such constructs. Lastly, the chapter explores the various options available for their control. An annex appended at the end of the chapter gives an overview of TNWs currently deployed around the world and of the systems employable for their delivery.

"TACTICAL" AND "STRATEGIC" IN CLASSICAL MILITARY THOUGHT

In classical military thought, the notions of "tactical" and "strategic" applied to function.[1] Strategy referred to the art of planning and conducting a sequence of operations, possibly consisting of several battles and extending over more than one theatre, as a coherent and consistent whole that led to overall victory. Tactics, in contrast, referred to the art of executing plans and handling forces in battle to triumph in a military engagement. Thus, in the classical theory of warfare, strategy and tactics were generally assumed to have different meanings. Strategy was understood as the general plans of how to achieve the aims of war, whereas tactics were understood as the specific ways of employing forces and weapons to win a battle. In short, in classical military thought, the distinction between strategic and tactical turned on the functional level of warfare to which each concept applied.[2]

The original sin leading to a distorted understanding of "tactical" occurred between the two world wars. Enthusiasts of the newly discovered means of warfare, the aeroplane, believed that air warfare would be the way out of the carnage that the First World War had been.[3] Air war theorists like Italian General Douhet and United States General Mitchell saw bomber aeroplanes as capable of striking targets in-depth behind enemy forces—i.e. lines of communications, command posts, industrial centres and populated agglomerations—and thereby as having war-ending "strategic" functions. By carrying the war with devastating consequences to the most valued assets of the enemy, it was surmised that the will of the enemy would be quickly broken, and victory would be shortly achieved. In other words, by attacking the enemy's core value targets, air warfare would reach the strategic dimension of war from the outset without the labours of protracted battles, long marches, logistical nightmares, millions of dead soldiers, and

---

[1] Encyclopaedia Britannica, http://www.britannica.com.

[2] Edward N. Luttwak, *Strategy: The Logic of Peace and War*, Cambridge, Mass.: Harvard University Press, 1987.

[3] A similar approach was pursued by the enthusiasts of tank warfare, such as Guderian, Fuller, de Gaulle, or Liddell Hart.

all the rest that previous military engagements entailed.[4] The emergence of air war theory in the inter-war years introduced a vastly different idea of the methods and means by which the "strategic effect" of war might be reached. At the basis of this idea was the belief that the special characteristics of the bomber aeroplane, including its long reach, would allow one to compress strategy and tactics into a single dimension of warfare. In this regard, considerations of weapons' range emerged as a key concern in the execution of function. Later, however, in the early development of nuclear doctrine, such considerations led to a whole shift in military thought as distance alone became the sole characteristic distinguishing between "strategic" and "tactical".

TNWs IN HISTORICAL PERSPECTIVE

TNWs in the Cold War: Concepts and Capabilities

"Strategic bombing" in the Second World War did not quite live up to expectations. In the "Battle of Britain", strategic bombing conducted by Germany failed dismally. Allied bombing against Germany and Japan was devastating, but it did not break the morale of the population. The war was won only after the laborious three-front land campaigns in the Soviet Union, Italy and the western front in Europe, and the costly and bloody advance across the islands and on the sea in the Pacific. The atomic bombs were only used when Japan was largely defeated.[5]

The nuclear weapon appeared, in Bernard Brodie's words, as "the absolute weapon".[6] As a consequence, Brodie expected an end to major warfare. His vision was one of some sort of strategic, minimum deterrence. The threat of harsh, completely destructive retaliation in case

---

[4] David MacIsaac, "Voices from the Central Blue: The Air Power Theorists", in Peter Paret, *Makers of Modern Strategy from Macchiavelli to the Nuclear Age*, Princeton: Princeton University Press, 1986, pp. 624-647.

[5] David MacIsaac, *Strategic Bombing in World War II: The Story of the US Strategic Bombing Survey*, New York/London: Garland, 1976.

[6] Bernard Brodie, *The Absolute Weapon. Atomic Power and World Order*, New York: Harcourt Brace and Co., 1946.

of attack, would mean the end of war. The realm of the tactical would thus disappear. The notion of TNWs was alien to this line of thought. Nuclear war would be unambiguously strategic from the outset, in the sense used by the inter-war air strategists. Nuclear strategies, though, developed in a different direction.[7]

At the outset of the Cold War, in both Europe and East Asia, the United States faced a similar problem. In Europe, Soviet conventional forces—later reinforced by Soviet allies—were stationed in massive numbers in eastern Germany and its neighbours. In Korea, the United States perceived the threat of a coalition between the Democratic People's Republic of Korea (DPRK), the People's Republic of China (PRC) and the Soviet Union. We neither endorse nor refute this threat assessment. We merely recall it to help understand what motivated the evolution of a nuclear strategy in which TNWs played such a prominent role.

The initial United States reaction to these early Cold War circumstances was enunciation of the doctrine of massive nuclear retaliation. This amounted to a United States threat to respond to any Soviet or Soviet-sponsored conventional attack with an all-out nuclear strike against the Soviet homeland. It was not perfectly clear whether the United States *would* actually respond in this way—maybe the attack would be stopped by other means—but the threat of massive retaliation made it possible that America *might* well do this. The precondition for a policy of massive retaliation, was the invulnerability of the United States homeland to a Soviet counter-attack in kind. The absolute United States nuclear superiority that prevailed in the first decade of the nuclear age, however, did not last for too long. The successful launch of the first Soviet satellite Sputnik in 1957 indicated that the USSR was in possession of technology permitting it to build missiles of intercontinental range. Under the circumstances, massive retaliation lost credibility. A nuclear strike against the Soviet Union in response to an assault on Western Europe would invite reciprocal retaliation. Other means were thus called for to neutralize the Soviet conventional superiority.

---

[7] Lawrence Freedman, *The Evolution of Nuclear Strategy*, 2. ed., Basingstoke: Macmillan, 1989.

Neither in Europe nor on the Korean Peninsula were the United States and its allies willing to deploy conventional forces that would be strong enough to counter the perceived threat. Instead, nuclear weapons were thought to present a cheap answer to the problem of conventional inferiority. When the United States itself became vulnerable to a possible nuclear counter-strike—from the mid-1950s onward—the distinction between "strategic" and "tactical" nuclear weapons began to emerge. Even before the "Sputnik shock", thousands of shorter range nuclear weapons had already begun to be deployed in Europe under the "Radford plan", initially as another plank in the strategy of "massive retaliation" though ultimately pre-empting the setting of United States nuclear vulnerability.[8]

It is noteworthy that these short-range nuclear weapons were initially designed to operate as another instrument of massive retaliation. That is, their purpose was not so much military in nature as it was political. Massive retaliation was first and foremost a strategy aimed at the political deterrence of war. In case of failure, the implementation of massive retaliation would have meant the immediate escalation of war to the "strategic" end stage. In this sense, the employment of short-range nuclear weapons under massive retaliation would have been aimed not at gaining battlefield advantages but rather as part of the immediate termination of hostilities. In that, the difference from long-range weapons was close to nil.

From the 1960s, however, as the doctrine of massive retaliation elapsed, a curious change of perspective began to take hold in the parlance of nuclear terminology as the difference between "strategic" and "tactical" came to be exclusively defined by range. But range, strangely enough, was not defined from the perspective of the actor conducting the strategy, in this case, the United States. If strategic had meant the ability to reach the territory of the Soviet Union, then intermediate-range weapons stationed in Germany or Turkey (such as bombers, the Jupiter missiles of the 1950s/1960s, and the Pershing and cruise missiles of the 1980s) should have counted as strategic, but they

---

[8] Campell Craig, *Destroying the Village: Eisenhower and Thermonuclear War*, New York: Columbia University Press, 1998.

did not. The notion of range that was adopted by the United States and that was eventually codified in the Strategic Arms Limitation and Arms Reduction Treaties (SALT and START) was defined in terms of which Soviet nuclear weapons were capable of reaching the territory of the United States. For intercontinental ballistic missiles (ICBMs), this was a distance exceeding 5,500 km; for submarine-launched ballistic missiles (SLBMs), no such distance was defined as the subs could silently move close to the enemy's coastline before unleashing their arsenal. For bombers, definitions remained disputed for several systems—notably the Soviet Backfire—due to the flexibility and adaptability of bomber range. The principle, however, was clear: bombers were counted as strategic if they could make a round-trip sortie from and back to one's homeland, or if they were equipped to carry cruise missiles with a range exceeding 600 km. Also, the subsumption of sea-launched cruise missiles (SLCMs) was disputed. These weapons, in which the United States enjoyed an advantage for most of the Cold War, were considered by the Soviets to be strategic, but the United States sought to exempt them from the SALT and START agreements. Ad hoc solutions were employed to address this dispute.[9]

Current Status of TNWs

TNWs and Current NATO Military Doctrine

Meanwhile, a panoply of nuclear weapons had been fielded in Europe some of which could claim to be proper tactical weapons even under a classical definition, as they were meant to affect the situation on the battlefield. The logic of these deployments was evident. If nuclear weapons were meant to be a counter to Soviet conventional superiority, then these weapons had to be usable in battle in order to neutralize this superiority if war ever came. The variety of TNWs deployed throughout the Cold War was astonishing:

---

[9] Joseph Goldblat et al., *Arms Control. A Guide to Negotiations and Agreements*, London: Sage, 1994, p. 59.

- Nuclear landmines also called "Atomic Demolition Munitions" (ADMs) to destroy "hardened" targets such as large military and civil structures;
- Smaller landmines operated by special forces designed to sabotage the communication lines of the enemy in the rear;
- Several kinds of gravity bombs deployed on aeroplanes of various operational ranges to be dropped close to the battlefield or far in the depth of enemy lines;
- Air-to-air missiles (AAAs) to be used for defence against mass aircraft attacks;
- Air-to-surface missiles (ASMs) designed to penetrate even deeper behind enemy lines, and with less risk of interception;
- Nuclear artillery shells known as artillery-fired atomic projectiles (AFAPs) to be used against concentrations of mechanized enemy forces, which were more accurate and less susceptible to bad weather than aircraft-delivered bombs;[10]
- Missiles of short and intermediate ranges, the last generation of which—the Pershing II—could actually reach Moscow from launch sites in West Germany;
- Land-, air- and sea-based cruise missiles, whose ranges also enabled them to hit targets in the Soviet Union;
- Anti-submarine warfare (ASW) munitions; and
- Nuclear-tipped torpedoes.[11]

The variety of TNWs deployed in East Asia was less extensive, due to the smaller spaces which narrowed ranges of operations anyway. Yet

---

[10] These included the notorious "Davy Crockett" artillery rocket whose name was meant to honour the gallant Westerner who gave his life consciously and without a chance of escape or victory in the heroic defence of the Alamo at the outset of the American-Mexican war. These rockets were meaningful in their suicidal connotations in that their firing crews had a fair chance of dying from their own action, if not already from the blast, then from the fallout of these too powerful, too short-range weapons.

[11] The variety of tactical nuclear weapons deployed at the height of the Cold War is documented in William M. Arkin, Thomas B. Cochran and Milton M. Hoenig, *Nuclear Weapons Databook I. US. Forces and Capabilities*, Cambridge, Mass.: Ballinger, 1983; see also Chuck Hansen, *US Nuclear Weapons*, Arlington: Orion, 1988.

missiles, nuclear artillery shells and gravity bombs were deployed, and nuclear weapons deployed by the United States navy, notably as part of its aircraft carrier groups, were also available.

On the Soviet side, a similar arsenal emerged. In some regards, Soviet thinking on TNWs was similar to that of NATO. According to official scenarios, if NATO were to initiate war, nuclear weapons would be used to stop the Western offensive. In reality, however, in addition to their declared purpose TNWs were also slated to support offensive operations by Warsaw Pact conventional forces by opening gaps in NATO defences through which Soviet and allied forces could move.

The current reader will note an air of irreality surrounding all of this. Yet, at the time, such planning was taken very seriously by the militaries of both sides. For NATO in particular, the problem of "extended deterrence" posed vexing problems of credibility. Could the United States actually be expected to extend a "nuclear umbrella" over its allies when it risked the spectre of annihilation by a devastating Soviet counter-attack? Could it be expected, as the popular formulation went, "to sacrifice New York for Hamburg"? This dilemma was at the heart of the strategy of flexible response, introduced and pushed through in the 1960s against considerable initial resistance from the European allies by the then Secretary of Defence, Robert McNamara. The shift from massive retaliation to flexible response contributed considerably to the blurring of the divide between "tactical" and "strategic". Since flexibility implied a vast range of possible nuclear operations depending on the specific war situation, a vast array of TNWs was needed to deal with the different contingencies.

The intra-alliance politics of TNWs were considerably affected by the shift in United States nuclear doctrine to flexible response. Under flexible response, American and European interpretations of the role of TNWs began to differ markedly. For the Americans, the mission of TNWs under flexible response became truly tactical indeed—to give the defence battlefield advantages that would obviate the conventional superiority of the Warsaw Pact. The Europeans who were slated to provide the battlefield, however, felt less sanguine about this development.

To resolve the emerging nuclear dilemma, NATO developed two different interpretations of the flexible response missions of TNWs, one that satisfied United States needs and one that mitigated European fears. The United States-acceptable version was that TNWs presented a firebreak between conventional war and a "strategic" (intercontinental) nuclear exchange. In other words, the use of nuclear weapons in response to a conventional attack no longer necessarily implied the automatic escalation of conflict to the intercontinental level. Rather, TNWs confined to the battlefield would give the Soviets a hint of the coming strategic nuclear confrontation, thereby convincing them to stop their aggression. The European-acceptable version, in contrast, was that there existed a seamless web of deterrence in which TNWs played the role of the intermediate steps and that would lead from the first conventional bullet fired across the iron curtain to cataclysmic nuclear war and therefore, the European reasoning went, war would never start in the first place. Flexible response, in European eyes, was nothing else than a latter-day version of massive retaliation, and TNWs were still equivalent in their mission to "strategic" nuclear weapons![12]

To enhance European confidence in the nuclear guarantee, the United States and its NATO allies devised a system of nuclear sharing. European delivery systems (aircraft, artillery pieces and missile launchers) were designed and equipped for nuclear employment, and their crews were trained accordingly. The ordnance for these systems remained in strict United States custody, to be transferred only when the United States President—after consultation in the NATO Council—would authorize release.[13] This arrangement is nowadays under fire from non-NATO Nuclear Non-Proliferation Treaty (NPT) parties who assert that the obligations of the NPT not to transfer nuclear weapons (nuclear-weapon states (NWSs) commitment) and not to receive them (non-nuclear

---

[12] David N. Schwartz, *NATO's Nuclear Dilemmas*, Washington, D.C.: Brookings, 1983; and Leon V. Sigal, *Nuclear Forces in Europe. Enduring Dilemmas, Present Prospects*, Washington, D.C.: Brookings, 1984.

[13] Dieter Mahnke, *Nukleare Mitwirkung. Die Bundesrepublik Deutschland in der Atlantischen allianz 1954-1970*, Berlin/New York: De Gruyter, 1972.

weapon States (NNWSs) commitment) cannot be invalidated by the outbreak of war (see discussion below).[14]

In the intricate argumentation of extended nuclear deterrence, TNWs assumed a symbolic importance for the cohesion of the western Alliance that went much beyond their (doubtful) military value. Admiral Stanley Turner, former Director of the Central Intelligence Agency (CIA), recounts two examples of the aberrations of NATO nuclear strategy. He reports on plans to use air-delivered TNWs to destroy a bridge in Bulgaria that was too small to show on an aerial photograph. Further, he reports on another episode where the commander of the United States Cavalry regiment tasked with protecting the "Fulda Gap"—one of the likely axes of advance through West Germany by Soviet forces—proposed to use conventional weapons instead of the nuclear mines assigned to him to seal the Fulda valley; he had found through simulation and exercise that the conventional option was more efficient in achieving the defence mission. For this, he was badly reprimanded by his superiors. For the sake of Alliance cohesion, the use of nuclear weapons was not to be questioned, even if it made little military sense.[15]

As the integration of shorter-range nuclear weapons into NATO arsenals evolved, the meaning of "tactical" tended to revert towards its classical origin. TNWs were to be employed to win battles rather than to decide the outcome of the war at once. Sure, the signal emanating from the use of TNWs was meant to influence the course of the war as a whole, that is, to dissuade the enemy from continuing hostilities. But to engender this effect, these weapons had to be usable on the battlefield. The assignment of combat roles to TNWs, however, appears never to have influenced their definition within NATO or in the United States. SALT, which, as stated above, contains the most authoritative definition of "strategic" (and by default "tactical") was concluded much after NATO doctrine had incorporated tactical nuclear war-fighting scenarios.

---

[14] As reported by Rebecca Johnson, *Non-Proliferation Treaty: Challenging Times*, ACRONYM No. 13, London: ACRONYM Institute, 2000.

[15] Stansfield Turner, et al., *Caging the Nuclear Genie: An American Challenge for Global Security*, Boulder, CO.: Westview, 1997.

Does the Definition of TNWs on the Basis of Range Make Sense?

To define TNWs in terms of range is an outgrowth of historical incidence or, more precisely, of American doctrinal influence. How hollow the concept was came to the fore very clearly during the Cuban missile crisis. Whatever the complex international, domestic and military considerations on either side that led to the crisis might have been, one decisive trigger was concern in the Soviet Union about the United States Jupiter missiles deployed in Turkey. With a "tactical" range of about 2,800 km, they threatened essential targets in the Soviet Union. Soviet missile deployments in Cuba served to level the playing field. The SS4s that were deployed on the Caribbean island had a sub-strategic range as well. They constituted actually the Soviet answer to the United States nuclear deployments in Europe. Stationing nuclear weapons in Cuba gave the Soviet Union the ability to strike the territory of the United States without the use of intercontinental weapons. In the Cuban missile crisis, thus, weapons that were thought to be "tactical" by both sides, assumed a most significant "strategic" meaning. It is a terrible irony that the incident that brought the world closest to nuclear war ever was not a "strategic" stand-off, and not the escalation of conflict from the tactical (European) to the strategic (intercontinental) level, but rather TNWs turned to strategic missions.[16]

The case of the Cuban missile crisis points to a fact that is very important in a global perspective: the distinction between "tactical" and "strategic" nuclear weapons is very much in the eye of the beholder. The distinction is utterly relative. It depends on both the range of the weapons concerned, and on the targets they are intended to strike. Thus, during the Cold War, Soviet weapons that, due to their range, appeared tactical from the United States vantage point seemed to be highly strategic from the European perspective, as these threatened the whole set of assets and values dear to the European people. The distinction between the "theatre" area of Europe and the "strategic" transatlantic area as used in United States strategic discourse had an alarming ring to

---

[16] Marc Trachtenberg, *History and Strategy*, Princeton: Princeton University Press 1991, Chapter 6.

many Europeans, as if the fate of Europe was peripheral and the "real thing" was United States security. This interpretation was frequently heard in Europe in the flaring of anti-nuclear and anti-American feelings and the movements they evoked, notably in the early 1980s.[17]

If in the context of Cold War Europe (and as witnessed in the Cuban missile crisis) the distinction between "tactical" and "strategic" seems problematic, in different regional contexts this distinction is even more dubious. Between the USSR/Russia and China, weapons with a range of 500-1,000 km can be said to already assume a "strategic" character as they would permit each side to target high-value sites in the other country. Between India and China, a range of 500 (Tibet to India) to 2,000 km (India to China) might also be called "strategic". Between Pakistan and India, a range of a few hundred kilometres could also be counted as "strategic". As the "war of the cities" between Iraq and Iran proved, in a hypothetical nuclear duel between those two Persian Gulf countries, the Scud missile (300 km range) would assume strategic meaning, as its range would suffice to annihilate major urban agglomerations on both sides. Between Israel and Syria, less than 100 km would be enough to make weapons "strategic". Damascus is within 50 km of the Golan, and most major Israeli cities are easily within ranges of 150-300 km from Syrian launch points. In fact, one could argue that longer-range weapons of mass destruction-tipped ordinary artillery rockets must be counted as "strategic" weapons in the Middle East. On the Korean peninsula, similar considerations apply. Seoul is less than 50 km from the demilitarized zone that demarcates the border between the two Koreas. Nowadays, to the South Koreans even mid- and long-range artillery placed just north of the demilitarized zone counts as "strategic" weapons.

The conclusion of the preceding discussion is quite clear. There are two meanings of "tactical" that have developed in the course of the nuclear age. One relates to range and has its origins in the theory articulated by the inter-war strategic air-war thinkers. This meaning has

---

[17] Harald Müller and Thomas Risse-Kappen, "Origins of Estrangement: The Peace Movement and the Changed Image of America in West Germany", *International Security*, Vol. 12, No. 1, Summer 1987, pp. 52-88.

been used since early in the Cold War to distinguish between "tactical" and "strategic" nuclear weapons. The other relates to function (i.e. affects the course of battle) and is associated with the classical understanding of the term. This meaning evolved later in the United States along with nuclear war-fighting doctrines, but did not seem to exert any subsequent influence on the definition of TNWs.

VARIATIONS OF DEFINITIONS FOR TNWS

Besides the term "tactical", nuclear weapons other than those deemed to be strategic have been described by a variety of other expressions. A summary of these expressions and of their definitional criteria (mostly related to range) is presented below.

"Non-strategic" nuclear weapons encompass all nuclear weapons incapable of travelling the distance between the United States and the USSR, without implying what their use may be.

"Intermediate-range" nuclear weapons referred to the Pershing II and the ground-launched cruise missiles (GLCMs) that were deployed in Europe following the NATO double-track decision in 1979, and that had a range of 500 to 5,500 km. The term indicated that the use of these weapons could vary between "tactical" (battlefield-related) and "strategic" (core-value related) missions. Either of them was capable of reaching core targets in the Soviet Union.

"Shorter-range" or "short-range" nuclear weapons delimit a vast category of nuclear weapons whose combat range is less than 500 km.

"Battlefield" nuclear weapons describe a category of nuclear weapons that are meant to affect the military situation on the battlefield. Since the depth of the battlefield has been extended considerably during the nuclear age, the exact meaning of this term has remained fluent, although, given its emphasis on mission, it probably comes closest to the classical understanding of "tactical". When initially introduced, battlefield nuclear weapons probably comprised weapon systems such as artillery shells and rockets. Today, they may encompass anything up to intermediate-range weapons.

"Theatre" nuclear weapons are a comprehensive term which includes every type up to and including intermediate-range weapons. The term embodies the notion that it would be possible to fight a nuclear war within the confines of a geographical area only. During the Cold War, this idea was averse to Europeans and Soviets alike, as it could create the illusion in the United States that the first use of nuclear weapons might not lead to global catastrophe. On the other hand, the term reflected precisely the notion of a "fire wall" between the European theatre of war and an intercontinental nuclear exchange that was at the roots of the continued nuclear guarantee extended by the United States to Europe under the conditions of vulnerability to Soviet strategic weapons.

"Sub-strategic" nuclear weapons are a French term that describes the role shorter-range nuclear weapons play in French nuclear doctrine. Since its inception, France has rejected the philosophy of flexible response as advanced by the United States. While recognizing the prerogative of an option of nuclear employment short of an all-out attack against enemy territory, France thought it dangerous to involve nuclear weapons in the battlefield calculus. In French doctrine, sub-strategic (or pre-strategic) nuclear weapons were to serve the exclusive purpose of advertising to the enemy that all-out attack was impending. For this purpose, the employment of sub- or pre-strategic nuclear weapons had to be swift and impressive, but not target enemy territory (although targets in the "hinterland" of the enemy were not to be excluded). This conviction that nuclear deterrence rests on some residual flexibility between a conventional battle and an all-out nuclear cataclysm has now become common among NWSs. However, currently, "tactical" or "sub-strategic" nuclear weapons are no longer thought to be a necessary instrument for this residual flexibility. The United Kingdom, for instance, is currently planning to employ some of its "strategic" Trident-D-5 missiles—presumably outfitted with a single warhead only—for missions falling below the level of a concentrated attack against the core value targets of an enemy.

Is a Definition Needed?

Does it make sense to develop a new definition of TNWs? As has been shown, a definition based solely on range neglects the fact that many such weapons could in fact also assume a strategic mission. A more precise distinction between "tactical" and "strategic" weapons would thus also take account of the weapons' mission aspect. A more exact definition of TNWs would consider both the range and function of the weapons. A drawback to this approach, however, is that the same weapon system might be classified as tactical in one region and strategic in another. If the aim of the new definition is to serve in arms control negotiations, the resulting "duality" of weapon systems would severely complicate matters.

To avoid the duality dilemma, it has been suggested that the yield of a weapon could instead be used as the criterion of distinction. Generally speaking, strategic weapons are expected to have a larger yield than tactical ones. However, that is hardly always the case. For instance, modification 3 of the B61 warhead used by the United States for tactical purposes can have a yield of up to 170 kt, whereas modification 7 used for strategic purposes can have a yield as low as 10 kt. Because the precision of a weapon may affect the yield necessary to achieve its mission—the higher the delivery precision, the lower the necessary yield—yield and delivery precision considerations could be combined to arrive at a more accurate definitional criterion for TNWs. This option, however, would also lead to arms control difficulties because advanced conventional weapons delivery systems are often capable of carrying both conventional and nuclear warheads, and might thus be indistinguishable from nuclear ones. The same difficulty would arise if the function of a weapon alone were chosen as a definitional criterion.

A third possible option for defining TNWs would be to use the character of the forces with which the weapons are deployed as a definitional standard. As such, nuclear weapons deployed with general purpose forces would be called "tactical", while those operated by a special "nuclear" unit would be called "strategic".[18]

Whatever definitional criteria are chosen, there will always be difficulties in the classification of TNWs. The main issue in defining TNWs is to consider the purpose of the definition, for it is this which will

---

[18] We owe this observation to Nicolai Sokov.

determine whether or not the definition makes sense. The reason for this study is the concern that the United States-Soviet unilateral reductions achieved thus far might be reversed with the consequence that the whole regime might collapse.[19] An urgent task is therefore to codify the existing achievements into a treaty. For this purpose, a precise definition does not have a high priority. It would make more sense to explicitly list those systems that should be included into a treaty on reductions. All nuclear weapons that have not yet been covered by an arms control treaty should be considered. A more provocative definition based on the reason that further reduction and nuclear arms control are needed would therefore be that TNWs are those types of nuclear weapons that are not yet covered by an arms control treaty. It is in this sense that we use the term in the rest of this paper.

TNWs in Present NATO Doctrine[20]

NATO nuclear doctrine has evolved considerably since the end of the East-West conflict. The numbers and the variety of the nuclear arsenal have been remarkably reduced. Today, NATO retains only a single type of nuclear weapon in Europe, gravity bombs to be delivered by aircraft. Some 150 of these bombs have been reported to be deployed in six European countries, although it is not entirely clear whether they are actually stored in all these States. (For a detailed overview see the appendix: Types, Delivery Systems and Locations of TNWs.) Nevertheless, air force units in these countries are assigned the mission of carrying the TNWs to their targets in case of war if the release decision is made.

While aircraft armed with nuclear bombs offer flexibility in terms of range and targets, the removal and elimination of short-range battlefield nuclear weapon systems have no doubt reduced flexibility and

---

[19] See contribution by Wilson C. Potter, "Tactical Nuclear Weapons: The Nature of the Problem", in this volume.

[20] David S. Yost, *The US and Nuclear Deterrence in Europe*, Adelphi Papers 326, London: IISS, 1999 and Bruce Tertrais, *Nuclear Policies in Europe*, Adelphi Papers 32 , London: IISS, 1999.

downsized the number of scenarios in which the use of nuclear weapons would be conceivable. The sub-strategic arsenals of both France and Britain have also shrunk. Britain retains one single system in its strategic submarine forces, the Trident D-5; in exceptional circumstances, Britain would consider using this system for sub-strategic missions. France has a clear division of labour between its strategic submarines and its sub-strategic air-launched, land- and sea-based stand-off missiles. Paris has dismantled all other sub-strategic systems.

With lower numbers and less variety—and consequently diminished flexibility of use—TNWs have lost their central place in NATO war plans. Since the original rationale for having TNWs—the conventional superiority of the Warsaw Pact—has disappeared with the Pact itself, this change should not be surprising. Contrary to previous times, it seems that today a detailed and precise doctrine of nuclear deployment and employment no longer exists. NATO thus appears to have discarded a comprehensive analysis and discussions of situations in which nuclear weapons might be used, for what purpose, in what numbers and against which possible targets. This lack of precision planning is a clear shift from past practice, although it has always taken some time to move from a principled decision to operative military planning.

In its new strategic concept, NATO has declared the use of nuclear weapons to be "extremely remote", thus relegating these weapons to a more or less purely political role. Today NATO's remaining TNWs serve to maintain the façade of "nuclear sharing", symbolizing joint risks among allies and justifying the participation of the Alliance NNWSs in nuclear decision-making. The Nuclear Planning Group, once one of the most central and busy bodies in the NATO structure, can hardly find issues to occupy itself with nowadays.

However, a note of caution is in order. NATO has retained the option of using nuclear weapons first in war, in line with United States policy of not ruling out a nuclear response to a biological or chemical weapons attack. In addition, the way the NATO strategic concept is formulated indicates that the Alliance does not preclude the possibility of employing nuclear weapons even in a purely conventional contingency.[21] This causes some difficulties with regard to the NATO adoption of new tasks such as out-of-area missions for crisis management, peace enforcement and peacekeeping, which creates the unfortunate hypothetical scenario of the Alliance using nuclear weapons in non-self-defence situations.

RISKS INHERENT IN TNWS

The preceding discussion has already identified some specific risks connected to TNWs that make it advisable to subject them to strict internationally agreed rules, to reduce them to a minimum or to eliminate them altogether, to have them stored until elimination under strict verification and safety and security measures, and to establish complete transparency in this field. In this regard the following further considerations should also be added.

TNWs invite the development of a nuclear war-fighting mentality. Since their intended use is not that of the "absolute weapon", their utilization can be more readily contemplated. This, in turn, leads to the identification of missions for which the existing tactical arsenal might not suffice. A feedback dynamic between weapons types, missions, new weapon types and new missions ensues. TNWs hence mislead military planners into dealing with nuclear weapons as another ordinary means of warfare. The more normal the employment of such weapons appears, the lower the mental barriers blocking their use short of situations of national desperation.

Because they move with the troops to which they are assigned, TNWs are vulnerable to pre-emptive destruction. In a fast moving military engagement, the enemy may discover this movement and be alarmed that a nuclear strike is impending. It may then decide to attack these units to eliminate the nuclear risk. In a fast moving battle, the risk

---

[21] NATO Strategic Concept as reaffirmed in the Ministerial Meeting of the Defence Planning Committee and the Nuclear Planning Group, Final Communiqué, M-DPC/NPG-2(99) 157, Brussels, NATO, 2 December 1999, para. 6.

of being overrun is particularly great for troops with short-range weapons that are necessarily deployed close to the front line. In NATO parlance, "use them or lose them" was the slogan used to describe this scenario. The vulnerability of TNWs, thus, contains an inherent imperative to employ them early in warfare. Some have seen in this attribute a particular virtue, since the uncertainty and risk of early use add to their deterrent effect against the starting of war in the first place. TNWs epitomize the prescription of Thomas Schelling "to leave something to chance". Since so much can go wrong, miscalculation and panic on the part of the weapons bearers can mislead them into firing their TNWs even without objective tactical necessity. As such, the enemy would be well advised not to bring these troops into such dangerous situations in the first place and deterrence would obtain. This, however, is an overly risky calculation between enemies at close range, where skirmishes could occur and small-scale transgressions could escalate into broader engagements. The shortest-range TNWs especially are thus a factor of grave instability.

In order to evade the risk of detectable movement, weapons may be deployed with their operational forces all the time, and authority to fire them may be pre-delegated to local commanders. By proliferating the authority and technical capability to initiate a nuclear exchange, this arrangement enhances instability and the risk for misperception and miscalculation.

Some TNWs are quite small. They can be carried by one or two soldiers. They are thus much more susceptible to theft than more sizeable and heavy warheads. In addition, older TNWs do not have the sophisticated electronic locks—permissive action links—that were designed to prevent unauthorized use in more modern designs. In other words, certain types of TNW present a greater risk of unauthorized or even terrorist use.

TNWs could be used to neutralize progress in strategic nuclear disarmament. Presently, this possibility would appear remote. However, the Cuban missile crisis plays witness to the inherent dangers that so-called TNWs turned to strategic missions could engender. Aircraft with sub-strategic ranges fitted with stand-off missiles can embark on strategic missions with ease especially if in-flight refuelling is available, while the geographic deployment of other kinds of TNWs could render these usable towards strategic ends.

In addition, TNWs pose a true challenge to nuclear non-proliferation in a more general sense. The preamble of the NPT states as a basic objective of the Treaty the prevention of all nuclear war. TNWs are built to fight nuclear war. Their military objective is to escalate from other levels of warfare—conventional, biological or chemical—to the nuclear one. It is hard to see how this could be compatible with the aforementioned objective of the NPT. This question is all the more pressing in view of NATO's planned nuclear release procedures in case of war. To declare the NPT invalid when major war has broken out, and to justify the breach of its basic obligations—no transfer of nuclear weapons by NWSs and no acquisition of these weapons by NNWSs (Articles I and II)—obviate, again, the meaning of the preamble. Moreover, NATO's retention of the first-use option, embedded in its deployment of nuclear gravity bombs in Europe, is an unequivocal invitation to countries in harsher security environments to emulate this posture. If the strongest military power in the world needs this option—and the related weapons—to prevent war in general and respond in unnamed and unforeseeable contingencies, why should not everybody else?

Finally, TNWs may present, again on a general level, the most visible proof that the NWSs are not willing to proceed with nuclear disarmament. TNWs are meant for fighting nuclear war. They betray a willingness to consider the use of nuclear weapons to gain military advantage. This willingness is completely incompatible with a serious commitment to reduce nuclear weapons to zero, even over an extended period of time.[22]

---

[22] For a thorough treatment of this and other post-war nuclear issues, consult Tom Sauer, *Nuclear Arms Control: Nuclear Weapons in the Post-Cold War Period*, Basingstoke: Macmillan, 1998.

Conclusion

TNWs are clearly remnants of the Cold War. On the NATO side, the military and political circumstances that once led the Alliance to deploy these weapons in huge numbers have entirely disappeared. Here, *entirely* must be emphasized, for the present strategic situation—including that of new members—does not require the retention of a single one of these weapons in Europe. While during the Cold War both the United States nuclear guarantee and the specific form in which it was given were prerequisites for the relinquishment of national nuclear options by western European NNWSs, this is no longer the case. A change in the NATO nuclear posture would not engender high new proliferation risks.[23] From the Western perspective at least, this situation offers the opportunity for a review of doctrine and deployment policies, and, even more so, for considerations of arms control and disarmament possibilities for this particular category of weapons.

TNWs bear particular inherent risks and liabilities that make them appear even more dangerous and problematic than long-range nuclear weapons. These problems exist independent of what the strategic justification for their deployment may be. That the Russian Federation believes increasingly in the necessity of keeping such weapons—or even of producing more and new types—is well known. However, this belief does not obviate the principled and practical objections against the retention of TNWs. The risks are large, and remedies are needed.

For these reasons, it is advisable to think seriously about instruments conducive to the reduction or complete elimination of TNWs. Such instruments are be discussed in the last section of this paper.

It is in the nature of nuclear weapons that it is not easy to devise arms control approaches that are restricted to one particular region only. Long-range nuclear weapons evidently have global reach, and restrictions must thus apply on a global scale. TNWs play their role

---

[23] Harald Müller, *Kernwaffen und deutsche Interessen: Versuch einer Neubestimmung*, HSFK-Report, Frankfurt/M: HSFK, May 1999 (English version forthcoming).

within a given theatre, but they are easily and quickly transported and deployed over great distances. For this reason, a majority of the proposals that follow are designed taking into account the European as well as the global context.

What Can Be Done to Address the Problem?

A Global Prohibition

The farthest reaching measure would be to ban all TNWs worldwide. This could come about due to the assessment that this category of weapons—because of its specific inherent risk—makes nuclear war or nuclear terrorism so much more likely that a complete prohibition is in the interest of all.

While it is conceivable that such an agreement could be concluded on a bilateral basis, it is more likely that it would only become possible if all the NWSs were to participate. A ban would assume complete declaration of existing arsenals, and include some measures to verify the completeness of the declaration as well as the destruction of these stocks. The task of verifying the completeness of declarations should not be underrated. No doubt some form of challenge inspections would have to be considered in order to allay fears of clandestine stocks, although, one may wonder what the advantage of such stocks might be as long as strategic arsenals continued to exist. If strategic nuclear weapons were further reduced, however, such concerns might have some justification.

Whatever flexibility the NWSs would wish to retain in terms of selective use or pre-strategic usage on nuclear weapons, this would have to be supplied by their strategic arsenals. The United Kingdom having announced that Trident would substitute for the role of the air-delivered wing of the British nuclear arsenal, has demonstrated that such a solution is indeed feasible.

Deep Cuts and Upper Limits

Since the complete elimination of TNWs assumes a major change in existing doctrines and Alliance arrangements, they may face too much opposition in the short term. NATO may be loathe to renounce the embedded flexibility allowed by TNWs altogether, France may not wish to forego the pre-strategic options provided by its air-launched stand-off missiles, and Russia may feel that the weakness of its conventional forces would make the disappearance of shorter-range nuclear weapons a risk to national security.

If these objections obtain, an upper limit for TNW holdings could be a more realistic option. Such a limit might even be concluded on a bilateral basis. The question then is where this limit should be set. As a rule, fewer would be better, since the fewer TNWs are around, the fewer storage areas are maintained, the lesser the risks of theft or unauthorized use. An upper limit of a few hundred would be more than sufficient for all foreseeable scenarios. One hundred could be a salient number. It would be equally desirable to agree on the type of TNWs to be retained. The weapon of choice would likely be gravity bombs or stand-off air to ground missiles, as air delivery offers the greatest flexibility.

As in the case of a total prohibition, TNW stocks would have to be declared and surplus weapons eliminated under adequate verification. In addition, permanent storage sites would have to be declared and checked regularly to verify that only the permitted number of weapons was held in store. Provision for challenge inspections would reassure parties that retaining sites with clandestine holdings would present a risk of detection for the perpetrator.

A Quantitative Freeze

A more moderate measure would be to freeze the quantity of existing stockpiles. Parties would thus agree not to increase the number of existing TNWs. New production would only replace an equal number of existing warheads that were withdrawn due to ageing or technical defects.

In order to make such an agreement credible, participants would have to exchange information about the amounts and types of their existing stockpiles as well as about all replacement actions. Transparency and credibility would be enhanced if the freeze applied within each weapon category rather than for the gross number of weapons, as the latter type of agreement would permit countries to increase holdings in a certain category if stocks in another category were reduced accordingly.

Verifying a quantitative freeze of TNWs would not be impossible, but it would be intrusive. Warheads would presumably have to be tagged individually, and a permanent presence of inspectors at production site exits and storage site entries and exits might well be necessary to certify the existence of only properly accounted for warheads.

Prohibition of Certain Types

The inherent risks posed by TNWs vary with type. If a complete prohibition or a numerical limit turns out to be unfeasible due to the objections of certain States, prohibiting certain types of TNWs could still amount to a net gain in security. TNW types that because of their inherent characteristics would be particularly fit for theft or early use might be the favourite candidates for such a selective prohibition regime. The most striking examples are:

- Nuclear mines because they can be so easily carried away;
- Nuclear artillery shells, grenades and rockets and short-range ballistic missiles, for the same reason and because they are more susceptible to the "use them or lose them" imperative; and
- Nuclear anti-aircraft and anti-missile weapons because of the environmental damage (radioactive fallout) their use would cause.

Declarations and destruction under observation would be advisable. Whether more penetrating verification measures could be agreed to is more difficult to assess. Since this would only be a partial prohibition, such verification might meet objections for reasons of national security if no numerical limits on remaining nuclear weapons were set. In combination with the previous measure discussed, however, more intrusive verification would probably be possible.

Withdrawal/Deployment to NWS Territory Only

TNWs could be withdrawn to a few storage sites far removed from national borders, and be kept exclusively on the territory of NWSs. Russia could reciprocate a removal of the remaining NATO gravity bombs to the United States by consolidating its own tactical arsenal behind the Urals, in due distance from the Chinese border, however.

While the storage areas would not be inspected, some measure should be taken to ascertain the non-existence of TNWs in the areas where they would be off-limits. This could be done by following the model of, or even in combination with, the inspection scheme under the Conventional Forces in Europe (CFE) Treaty. Since this scheme is geared towards checking for the presence of "legal" holdings in declared sites, and the absence of illegal surplus holdings at those same sites, and of illegal holdings in non-declared sites, it is probably a useful framework for checking the withdrawal and non-deployment of TNWs.

This scheme, again, could be realized bilaterally (although with allied acquiescence on the American side).

Nuclear-Weapon-Free Zone (NWFZ)

The origin of the idea of establishing a NWFZ in Europe dates back to the 1950s, when it was known as the "Rapacki plan", named after the then Polish Minister of Foreign Affairs. The plan aimed, of course, at preventing the deployment of TNWs in Western Europe, notably West Germany, thereby perpetuating the conventional superiority of Soviet and Warsaw Pact forces in the region. It was thus fully rejected by NATO and its member States. Today, however, the situation is vastly different, with NATO fielding by far the stronger conventional forces and enjoying an unchallenged superiority. Nevertheless, despite such changed circumstances, a similar proposal recently brought forth by Belarus with Russian consent received little attention.

However, it is by no means clear that the creation of a NWFZ in central eastern Europe would be to the disadvantage of either NATO or its new members. This depends very much on the scope of the zone and the specific stipulations of the concomitant treaty. If, for example, such a zone were to include Sweden, Finland, the Baltic States, Belarus, Ukraine, Poland, Hungary, Eastern Germany (which is, by the Two plus Four Treaty nuclear weapon-free anyway), the Czech Republic, Slovakia, Bulgaria, and Romania, the Kaliningrad oblast and a strip of, say, 200 km east of the Russian western border, this would deprive the Russian Federation of the ability to deploy nuclear weapons in the immediate neighbourhood of potential new NATO members, thereby avoiding a situation such as during the Cold War when both alliances fielded TNWs literally in sight of each other. If, in addition, the validity of such a treaty were made contingent on the observation of other rules, such as the CFE Treaty, the Vienna Documents and the Paris Charter, then NATO would be authorized to bring nuclear weapons forward when a threat arose, for in order for Russia to assemble the necessary concentration of forces in forward areas for an aggression, these various agreements would have to be breached. It is reasonable to assume that everybody's security, not just Russia's, would be well served by such a cobweb of agreements. However, present NATO alliance politics make the achievement of a NWFZ close to impossible.

Prohibition of the Development of New Types of TNWs

A prohibition on the development of new types of TNWs would amount to a qualitative freeze of the status quo. The objective would be to prevent nuclear doctrine from evolving into ever more sophisticated war-fighting schemes, or to lower the threshold of nuclear weapons employment further. It is obvious that such an agreement would be strongly supported by the entry into force of the Comprehensive Test Ban Treaty (CTBT). Without actual testing, the modification of existing designs is certainly possible, but the development and certification of completely new types of TNW is unlikely.

In order to lend credibility to the obligations under a qualitative freeze, the parties would have to know something about each other's existing stocks. Information about the types of weapons in existing stockpiles would thus be necessary. The parties should also have the right to ask for clarification if they suspect that one of their partners is actually introducing a new type of TNW in violation of its commitments. All parties should be accountable, that is, have to answer a clarification request.

It is rather unlikely that such a prohibition agreement would be supported by intense verification. Since the limitations are qualitative and the existing stocks would continue to exist, on-site inspection may be excluded for fear of divulging security-relevant design information.

Transparency: A TNWs Register

TNWs could be covered by a register, a comprehensive transparency measure long advocated by Germany. A register would have to bring together data that would accompany, as discussed, a quantitative and qualitative freeze. It would contain information on the overall number of weapons held, their types, and the quantities of each type. In an even more comprehensive version, it might also specify the locations and the numbers/types held in each location. Such detail would require a considerable degree of mutual trust and faith in the peaceful intentions of one's partners. Otherwise, some States may fear that by giving away specifics about locations they would help potential enemies with targeting.

The register would be amended annually for additions and reductions, so that those participating would have a regularly updated overview of each other's stockpiles. Such a register would serve as a confidence-building measure—countries are unlikely to offer that much information if they are preparing a nuclear attack. A register would also be a useful tool in establishing a baseline for future disarmament measures, or in accompanying these measures as they go along.

To optimize the use of the register, participants could be given the right to pose questions and ask for clarifications, and accept the duty of accountability if so required.

Physical Security

As the physical security of TNWs is one main concern of those trying to put these weapons on the arms control and disarmament agenda, measures to address this subject directly may appear attractive to some. While it appears obvious that NWSs themselves share a keen interest in keeping their weapons as secure as possible, a consensus on common standards may provide welcome and useful reassurance. The following proposal uses the model of both the "Convention on the Physical Protection of Nuclear Materials" and the guidelines on the same subject issued by the International Atomic Energy Agency (IAEA) which establish standards for good practice, without compromising national security considerations by requiring intrusive verification measures. Countries, would of course, be free to establish practices stricter than those contained in the agreement.

Such an agreement may establish the obligation to equip all TNWs with electronic locks—permissive action links—that prevent unauthorized use and to withdraw weapons from stockpiles and dismantle them if they do not have these features and if it is impossible, too expensive or undesirable to change their design accordingly. A second obligation would be to keep only weapons with safe designs that are not prone to explode or fizzle as a consequence of accident. TNWs, thus, should contain insensitive chemical explosives and should be one-point safe. Thirdly, TNWs should be stored in secure storage sites, in locked vaults that cannot be easily penetrated. Fourthly, storage sites should be protected by armed guards, the reliability of which should be checked regularly. Countries should make it a crime, subject to strict penalties, to interfere or to plan to interfere with nuclear weapons. Similar strict rules must guide the transport of these devices, and their handling at the entry or exit of production facilities.

The agreement would provide for regular reports by the parties on actions taken to implement their treaty obligations. Reports should be specific enough for the partners to assess implementation, yet general enough to protect the security of the reporting State.

Doctrine/No-first-use

Constraints placed on nuclear doctrine inevitably have consequences for TNWs. The proposal to agree on an universally applicable no-first-use doctrine, as proposed by the People's Republic of China, would profoundly affect the justification for maintaining TNWs. It is very hard to see how, under a no-first-use doctrine, short-range nuclear weapons in huge numbers could serve a useful and legitimate purpose. In fact, it can be surmised that if nuclear weapons are only usable in response to a first use by another party, only long-range nuclear weapons, if possible in an invulnerable mode of deployment, would make any sense. If a no-first-use agreement is to be more than mere lip-service to a popular objective, it should be reflected in nuclear postures. A NWS subscribing to no-first-use will have a hard time justifying the continued possession of TNWs.

FINAL COMMENTS

Some of the proposals developed above are clearly mutually exclusive. A freeze, a limitation and a complete prohibition are alternatives, or stages following each other sequentially, but they cannot be achieved simultaneously. Other options can be combined. A prohibition fits well together with a no-first-use agreement. A freeze and a limitation can easily be complemented by a register, a limitation of types and a no-new-types treaty. Whatever measure is chosen, it should be optimized through a sensible combination of instruments.

One major problem that cannot be ignored is the status of the de facto NWSs, India, Israel and Pakistan. It is highly undesirable that these countries develop or retain nuclear weapons falling into the "tactical" category if such types are banned by legal instruments for the official NWSs. The issue is all the more difficult as weapons falling into the "tactical" category are "strategic" given the geo-strategic contexts of these countries, as discussed above.

Leaving these countries out is undesirable. Including them is as well undesirable if such inclusion can be construed as implying the recognition of their nuclear weapon status. This problem, already present in the efforts to establish cut-off negotiations (and even more so if these negotiations were to take off) applies here as well. It remains to be seen whether a disclaimer placed into the preambles or specific articles of the agreements-to-be negotiated would provide a cheap way out of this dilemma.

APPENDIX
TYPES, DELIVERY SYSTEMS AND LOCATIONS OF TNWS

TNWs show a lot of diversity. They range from some short-range weapons intended for tactical battlefield use (i.e. nuclear torpedoes), to others that have characteristics similar to strategic weapons (i.e. sea-launched ballistic missiles, SLBMs). In a number of cases, TNWs—having a larger yield and comparable delivery range—could fulfil strategic missions. In the following, all those systems that could be classified as TNWs, their locations and delivery systems, are compiled for the United States, Russia, the United Kingdom, France, China, India, Pakistan, and Israel.

UNITED STATES TNWS

Since the end of the Cold War, the number of United States TNWs has been reduced to 970 warheads—650 B61 bombs deployed on dual-capable aircraft, and 320 nuclear Tomahawk sea-launched cruise missiles (SLCMs), which are stored in depots in the United States for possible redeployment on attack submarines.[1] An overview is shown in Table 1.[2]

---

[1] G. Lewis, *Arms Control for Tactical Nuclear Weapons*, paper for 1998 Summer Symposium on Science and World Affairs, Cambridge, Mass., 14 July 1998.

[2] W. M. Arkin, R. S. Norris and J. Handler, *Taking Stock—World-wide Nuclear Deployments 1998*, Washington, D.C.: NRDC, 1998, Table 2, p. 14. (On p. 54, however, a larger number is given: 1,350 B61, 600 of them awaiting dismantlement at Pantex, and 320 W80-0.)

Table 1: United States TNWs (NRDC)

Type	Year first deployed	Range/ km	Warheads x yield	Warheads	Location
B61 Tactical Bombs mods- 3, -4, -10	1979	n.k	0.3-170 kt	650	USA, 150 in Europe
SLCM/W80-0	1984	2,500	5 and 150 kt	320	USA (storage)

Table 2 gives an overview of their location.[3]

Table 2: Locations of United States TNWs (NRDC)

Type	User	Number	Location (No. of warheads)
B61 Tactical Bombs mods -3, -4, -10	Air Force, NATO	1,350	Kirtland AFB, NM (600) (near Pantex dismantlement plant) Nellis AFB, NV (600) Europe (150)
SLCM/W80-0	1984	2,500	North Island, Ca (160) Yorktown, Va (160)

In Europe, United States TNWs are stationed in Kleine Brogel, Belgium; Büchel, Spangdalem and Ramstein, Germany; Araxos, Greece; Lakenheath, United Kingdom; Ghedi-Torre and Aviano, Italy; Volkel, the Netherlands; and Inçirlik, Turkey.

Descriptions of the systems are as follows:

---

[3] Ibid., p. 54.

The B61 Warhead[4]

The B61 comes in several modifications. Some modifications are out of service, others are used for strategic systems, and three are used for tactical purposes, i.e. mods 3, 4, and 10. An overview is given in Table 3.

Table 3: Features of individual models (FAS)

Modification	Yield	Notes
3	4 yield options - 0.3 kt, 1.5 kt, 60 kt, and 170 kt	Highest yield tactical bomb, microprocessor based arming and firing
4	0.3 kt, 1.5 kt, 10 kt, and 45 kt	Microprocessor based arming and firing
10	0.3 kt, 5 kt, 10 kt, and 80 kt	
11	Multiple yield options ranging from 10 kt to 340 kt.	For tactical and strategic use Underground explosion at 3-6 m. The actual warhead itself is identical to the Mod 7

As seen in the table, a tactical B61 can have a higher yield than a strategic one (i.e. the yield options of the strategic mod 7 range from only 10 to 340 kt). The B61 is a two stage radiation implosion weapon, which means that it is a hydrogen bomb that consists of a boosted fission primary based on the implosion principle and a thermonuclear secondary. The primary consists of beryllium reflected plutonium, the secondary of lithium-6 deuteride fusion fuel. The variable yield options can be dialled from the outside. The lowest yield, i.e. 300 tons, probably represents the basic unboosted yield of the fission primary. The B61 is

---

[4] Very detailed information on United States TNWs can be found on the web pages of the Federation of American Scientists (FAS). These pages are the main source for the technical descriptions presented in this appendix. For the B61 system see http://www.fas.org/nuke/hew/Usa/Weapons/B61.html.

designed for high-speed external carriage and low altitude delivery, and has a light weight of about 350 kg. It is equipped with several safety features, safeguards against accidents and unauthorized use.

The B61 is deliverable by any United States or NATO nuclear-capable aircraft including: B-52, B-1, B-2B, F-15E, F-16, F/A-18, and the Tornado (NATO).

Mod 11 is a modified Mod 7 with a one-piece case hardened steel centre case, and a new nose-piece and rear sub-assembly to provide ground penetration capability for defeating buried targets. It buries itself 3-6 metres underground before detonation, transferring a much higher proportion of the explosion energy to ground shock, compared to surface bursts. This is the first new model of a United States warhead to go into service since warhead production was suspended in 1989. Currently the B61-11 is deployed for use with the stealth B-2 bomber.

Delivery Systems for the B61[5]

B-1B Lancer[6]

The B-1B is a multi-role, long-range bomber, capable of flying intercontinental missions without refuelling and of penetrating sophisticated enemy defences. It can perform a variety of missions, including that of a conventional weapons carrier for theatre operations. Until 1991, the B-1 was assigned to a nuclear weapons delivery role. The B-1B enables aircrews to navigate globally without the need for ground-based navigation aids. The B-1B represents a major upgrade in United States long-range capabilities over the B-52—the previous mainstay of the American bomber fleet.

---

[5] An overview with links to detailed descriptions of United States systems can be found at http://www.fas.org/man/dod-101/sys/ac.

[6] See http://www.fas.org/nuke/guide/usa/bomber/b-1b.htm.

B-2 Spirit[7]

The B-2 is a multi-role bomber capable of delivering both conventional and nuclear munitions. Its stealth characteristics give it the ability to penetrate air defences. It has an intercontinental range without refuelling. The blending of low-observable technologies with high aerodynamic efficiency and large payload gives the B-2 important advantages over existing bombers.

B-52 Stratofortress[8]

The B-52H is the primary nuclear-tasked bomber in the United States Air Force (USAF) inventory. It provides the only air-launched cruise missile (ACLM) carrier in the USAF. The bomber is capable of flying at high subsonic speeds at altitudes up to 15,166.6 metres. It can carry nuclear or conventional ordnance and is capable of worldwide precision navigation. The use of aerial refuelling gives the B-52 an unlimited range. Unrefuelled, it has a combat range in excess of 14,080 km.

F-15 Eagle[9]

The F-15 is an all-weather, extremely manoeuvrable, tactical fighter-bomber designed mainly to gain and maintain air superiority in aerial combat. It is equipped with electronic systems and weaponry to detect, acquire, track and engage enemy aircraft operating over the horizon. Its weapons and flight control systems are designed so that one pilot can safely and effectively perform air-to-air combat. The identification "friend or foe" system informs the pilot if an aircraft seen visually or on radar is friendly. The F-15 can also be employed in an air-to-ground combat role and can be fitted with the B61 gravity bomb.

---

[7] See http://www.fas.org/nuke/guide/usa/bomber/b-2.htm.
[8] See http://www.fas.org/nuke/guide/usa/bomber/b-52.htm.
[9] See http://www.fas.org/man/dod-101/sys/ac/f-15.htm.

F-16 Fighting Falcon[10]

The F-16 is a compact, multi-role fighter-bomber aircraft designed for air-to-air and air-to-ground combat. In an air-to-air combat role, the F-16's manoeuvrability and combat radius (distance it can fly to enter air combat, stay, fight and return) exceed those of all potential enemy fighter aircraft. It can locate targets in all weather conditions and can detect low flying aircraft in radar ground clutter. In an air-to-ground role, the F-16 can fly more than 860 km and can be armed with the B61 gravity bomb. An all-weather capability allows it to accurately deliver ordnance during non-visual bombing conditions.

F/A-18 Hornet[11]

The F/A-18 is a single- or two-seat, twin engine, multi-mission fighter-bomber aircraft that can operate from either aircraft carriers or land bases. The F/A-18 fills a variety of roles: air superiority, fighter escort, suppression of enemy air defences, reconnaissance, forward air control, close and deep air support, and day and night ground strike missions. The F/A-18 Hornet replaced the F-4 Phantom II fighter and A-7 Corsair II light attack jet, and is also replacing the A-6 Intruder which was retired during the 1990s. The aircraft can carry the B61 gravity bomb.

Tornado[12]

Designed and built as a collaborative project in the United Kingdom, Germany and Italy, the Tornado is in service with all three air forces and the German Navy. It is a twin-seat, twin-engine, variable geometry aircraft and is supersonic at all altitudes. Originally the aircraft was intended for use in central Europe in armour interdiction and air superiority roles. Fitted with the B61 gravity bomb, the Tornado can also be deployed in a nuclear combat role.

---

[10] See http://www.fas.org/man/dod-101/sys/ac/f-16.thm.
[11] See http://www.fas.org/man/dod-101/sys/ac/f-18.thm.
[12] See http://www.fas.org/man/dod-101/sys/ac/row/tornado.htm.

The W80 Warhead and the SLCM[13]

The W80 warhead comes in two nearly identical modifications: mod 0 and mod 1. Its design is based on the B61. Similar to the B61, it is a two-stage radiation implosion weapon. The available yields range from 5 kt to 150 kt, its weight is about 130 kg. The 5 kiloton low yield option presumably represents the boosted primary yield alone, while the high yield adds the full secondary yield. The primary fissile material is plutonium.

The W80 arms three cruise missiles currently in the United States arsenal—the mod 0 arms the SLCM which is considered to be non-strategic, while the mod 1 arms the ALCM and the advanced cruise missile (ACM), both of which are considered to be strategic systems.

During the Cold War, the SLCM (Tomahawk Land Attack Missile—Nuclear, TLAM-N[14]) was carried aboard a variety of ships and submarines. Since September 1991, however, all SLCMs have been removed and have been placed in storage. The 320 systems are stored in depots in the United States for possible redeployment on attack submarines. The missile is launched with a solid fuel booster to provide it with initial impulse, which is subsequently jettisoned as the turbofan engine takes over. Its guidance system is similar to that of the ALCM, the missile being outfitted with a terrain contour matching (tercom) device.

During the 1980s the SLCM became known as the "fourth leg" of the United States nuclear triad to some. Given its long range and the forward deployment of United States naval forces, it did qualify as a strategic system.

RUSSIAN TNWs

Many types of Russian TNW do not have a United States counterpart.

---

[13] See http://www.fas.org/nuke/hew/Usa/Weapons/W80.html.

[14] Center for Defense Information (CDI), http://www.cdi.org/issues/nukef&f/database/usnukes.html.

Only little official information on the numbers of Russian TNWs is publicly available. Estimates therefore are based on a few official statements, United States intelligence reports and conclusions by experts. Consequently, estimates of Russian TNWs vary substantially.

Nikolai Sokov has estimated the following numbers (Table 4) of warheads which have been classified as tactical in the 1991/1992 initiatives:[15]

Table 4: Estimates of non-deployed Russian TNWs (Sokov)

Category	Total warheads by January 1998	Total in the spring of 1999
Land-based missiles	800	0
Artillery shells	400	0
Atomic demolition munitions (mines)	140	0
Air defence missiles	1,500	1,500
Tactical aviation	3,500	3,500
Naval weapons	3,400	3,400
Total	**9,740**	**8,400**

The Natural Resources Defence Council (NRDC) estimates that in addition to 4,000 deployed tactical warheads, another 12,000 could be in reserve, and/or awaiting dismantlement.[16]

---

[15] Nikolai Sokov, "Estimate of Total Russian (non-deployed) Sub-Strategic Nuclear Weapons," appendix to William C. Potter, "Update on Developments Regarding Tactical Nuclear Weapons Disarmament", presented to the United Nations Secretary-General's Advisory Board on Disarmament Matters, New York, 28-30 June 1999.

[16] W. M. Arkin, R. S. Norris and J. Handler, *Taking Stock—World-wide Nuclear Deployments 1998*, p. 27.

Three publicly available estimates on deployed warheads conclude that the number is around 4,000, but there are substantial variations in the categories. This illustrates the lack of transparency. The estimates are shown in Table 5.[17]

Table 5: Deployed Russian TNWs (NRDC, 1998)

Category/Type	Weapon System	Launchers	Warheads
Air defence missiles			
ABMs	SH-08 Gazelle (64), SH-11 Gorgon (36)	100	100
SAMs	SA-5B Gammon, SA-10 Grumble	1,100	1,100
Tactical aviation			
Bombers and fighters	Backfire (120), Fencer (280) (AS-4 ASM, AS-16 SRAM, bombs)	400	1,600
Naval weapons			
Attack aircraft	Backfire (70), Fencer (70) (AS-4 ASM, bombs)	140	400
SLCMs	S-N-9, SS-N-12, SS-N-19, SS-N-21, SS-N-22	–	500
ASW weapons	SS-N-15, SS-N-16, torpedoes	nk	300
Total			**4,000**

According to Sokov, the 100 warheads for anti-ballistic missiles (ABMs) and 800 warheads for naval weapons (SLCMs and anti-

---

[17] Ibid. The authors calculate a sum of 4,000 tactical warheads. However their count of tactical aviation warheads is ambiguous (1,000 or 1,600). This, in turn, makes the total sum ambiguous (3,400 or 4,000).

submarine warfare, ASW) have already been dismantled or are awaiting dismantlement.

Alexei Arbatov and Anatoli Diakov present different numbers in Table 6.[18]

Table 6: Deployed Russian TNW warheads as presented by Arbatov (1999), by Diakov (1998), and by NRDC (1998, Table 5)

Category	Arbatov's numbers	Diakov's numbers	NRDC's numbers
Air defence missiles	600	1,250	1,100
Atomic demolition munitions (mines)	200	0	0
Tactical aviation	1,000	2,060	1,600
Naval weapons	2,000	2,400	1,200
Total	**3,800**	**5,710**	**3,900**

The locations are listed in Table 7.[19]

---

[18] See Alexei Arbatov, "Deep Cuts and De-alerting: A Russian Perspective" in H. A. Feiveson (ed.), *The Nuclear Turning Point—A Blueprint for Deep Cuts and De-Alerting of Nuclear Weapons*, Washington D.C.: Brookings Institution, 1999, p. 320, and Anatoli Diakov, quoted in Nikolai Sokov, "Estimate of Total Russian (non-deployed) Sub-Strategic Nuclear Weapons".

[19] W. M. Arkin, R. S. Norris and J. Handler, *Taking Stock—World-wide Nuclear Deployments 1998*, p. 83.

Table 7: Locations of Russian TNWs (NRDC)

Category	Number	Location
Air defence and naval aviation		
Backfire (Air force)	120 aircraft	Moscow area
Backfire (Naval)	70 aircraft	Alekseyevka, Belaya, Murmansk, Shaykovka (SE of Smolensk), Sol'tsy, SE of St Petersburg
Fencer (Air Force)	280 aircraft	Voronezh, Northern MD, North Caucasus, Ural, Transbaikal, Far East
Fencer (Naval)	70 aircraft	
Naval		
SLCM	500	Abrek Bay (SE of Vladivostok), Rybachiy Peninsula, Severodvinsk, Severomorsk, St Petersburg area
Anti-submarine warfare	300	

Descriptions of the systems are as follows:

Air Defence Missiles[20]

SH-08 Gazelle

The SH-08 is a nuclear-armed endoatmospheric interceptor designed to intercept ballistic missile warheads in the atmosphere. The Gazelle is the second, terminal tier of the Moscow ABM defence system

---

[20] Unless otherwise indicated, the description of Russian TNWs presented here is based on information compiled by Center for Defense Information, http://www.cdi.org/issues/nukef&f/database/rusnukes.html.

aimed at intercepting incoming warheads evading the upper, exoatmospheric tier interceptor, the SH-11 Gorgon. The SH-08 has a range of 80 km and a yield of 10 kilotons. Sixty-four missiles are or were deployed around Moscow.

SH-11 Gorgon ABM

The SH-11 is an exoatmospheric interceptor with a range of 350 km and a yield of 1 megaton. SH-11 missiles constitute the first tier of the ballistic missile defences deployed around Moscow. The missile also has a limited anti-satellite capability against targets in low earth orbit.

SA-5B Gammon

The SA-5B has a range of 150 km and a yield of 25 kilotons. It was designated in the 1950s to counter high-altitude American air threats. The United States has long claimed that the SA-5B has an ABM capability (and was tested in this role in the 1970s), particularly given the sizeable 25 kiloton nuclear warhead it carries. The ageing SA-5 has increasingly been replaced by the SA-10 Grumble, however. Because of their age, the SA-5B Gammon warheads would be a prime candidate for elimination.

SA-10 Grumble

The SA-10 has a range of 45, 75, or 90 km. Its yield is unknown. It is capable of high-altitude interception of large air-to-surface cruise missiles, and even has a limited interception of short-range ballistic missiles capacity. In fact, it is alleged that the Russians tried to sell the SA-10 to the Israelis as just such a short-range ABM system. Many have compared the SA-10 to the United States Patriot system, a surface-to-air missile not optimized or designed for theatre ballistic missile defence, but with some capabilities in this area. During the Reagan administration, there was considerable controversy in the United States about the possible ABM capability of the SA-10.

Land-based Non-strategic Nuclear Munitions

AS-4 Kitchen ASM

The AS-4 is an air-to-surface missile with a range of 400 km and a yield of 1 megaton. Compared to today's cruise missiles, the AS-4 is large. It is designed for high-altitude launch, with a cruise altitude in excess of 15 km, followed by a steep terminal dive onto the target.

AS-16 Kickback SRAM

The AS-16 is a very fast short-range weapon designed principally to destroy enemy air defences. Its range is 200 km, its yield 350 kilotons. The Russians describe it as an analogue to the recently retired American short-range attack missile (SRAM). Little else is known about the AS-16.

Gravity Bombs

The yield of the tactical variants are 250 and 350 kilotons. They can be deployed on medium-range bombers, as well as strike aircraft.

Land-based Non-strategic Bombers and Fighters

Tu-22M Backfire (Tupolev)[21]

The Backfire is a long-range aircraft capable of performing nuclear strikes, conventional attack, anti-ship and reconnaissance missions. Its low-level penetration features make it a much more survivable system than its predecessors. Carrying either gravity bombs or AS-4/Kitchen air-to-surface missiles, it is a versatile strike aircraft, believed to be intended for theatre attack in Europe and Asia but also capable of intercontinental missions against the United States. The Backfire can be equipped with probes to permit in-flight refuelling, which would further increase its range and flexibility.

---

[21] See http://www.fas.org/nuke/guide/bomber/tu-22m.htm.

Su-24 Fencer[22]

The Fencer is an all-weather attack fighter-bomber comparable to the Tornado. It can carry missiles and gravity bombs, and is capable of in-flight refuelling.

Naval Non-Strategic

SS-N-9 Siren SLCM

The SS-N-9 has a range of 110 km and a yield of 200 kilotons. It is a relatively short-range anti-ship cruise missile. After launch, the missile climbs to about 100 metres and uses its radar to identify the target. Ten kilometres out, the missile begins a slow, terminal dive onto the target. Given the age of this system and the availability of the newer SS-N-22 Sunburns, the SS-N-9 (certainly the nuclear version at least) would be a likely candidate for elimination.

SS-N-12 Sandbox SLCM

The SS-N-12 Sandbox is a second generation Soviet cruise missile. It has a range of 550 km and a yield of 350 kilotons. In recent years it has been gradually replaced by the third generation SS-N-19 Shipwreck. The missile is launched by a solid-fuel booster and then switches to a turbojet which allows for supersonic flight.

SS-N-19 Shipwreck SLCM

The SS-N-19 Shipwreck is a third generation Russian anti-ship cruise missile system. It was the first Soviet vertically-launched cruise missile, designed to defeat the growing defences of United States carrier battle groups. It has a range of 550 km and a yield of 500 kilotons. Little is known about the missile, although it is thought to be similar to the SS-N-12 Sandbox. The SS-N-19 is launched by a solid fuel booster, which

---

[22] See http://www.fas.org/man/dod-101/sys/ac/row/su-24.htm.

is jettisoned, and then cruises at an altitude of over 20 km, followed by a terminal dive onto the target.

SS-N-21 Sampson SLCM

The SS-N-21 has a range of 3,000 km and a yield of 200 kilotons. It is very similar to the United States SLCM, the Tomahawk TLAM-N. It can be fired from a conventional torpedo tube, with the wings expanding after it breaks the surface. It is initially powered by a solid fuel booster which is jettisoned, and then by a turbofan engine. The missile very likely has a theatre strike role.

SS-N-22 Sunburn SLCM

The SS-N-22 Sunburn is a follow-on to the SS-N-9 Siren. It has a range of 120 km and a yield of 200 kilotons. This short-range anti-ship weapon has many improvements over the SS-N-9, particularly its sea-skimming flight profile, lighter weight, improved accuracy and supersonic speed. The postulated main role of the SS-N-22 is to destroy the Aegis command/defence system-equipped vessels guarding United States carrier battle groups. The very high speed and sea-skimming flight profile would reduce time for the target to detect and launch defensive missiles. After a launch assisted by a solid fuel booster, the Sunburn cruises at approximately 20 metres altitude. The missile has its own active radar seeker, with improved jamming resisting capabilities.

SS-N-15 Starfish ASW

The SS-N-15 Starfish is a rocket-propelled nuclear depth bomb reportedly copied from a similar United States design. It can be fired from Russian 53 or 60 centimetre torpedo tubes. In fact, the SS-N-15 and SS-N-16—the former a nuclear depth charge and the latter a nuclear-tipped torpedo—were considered to be complementary weapon systems, and both types were jointly assigned to Russian submarines. The weapon is fired from a torpedo tube, then a rocket booster carrying the weapon to the vicinity of the target, ignites. The Starfish releases a 200 kiloton nuclear depth charge, which detonates at the optimum depth, likely destroying submarines in a 5-10 kilometre radius.

SS-N-16 Stallion ASW

Very little is known about the SS-N-16 Stallion. It is a short-range, submarine-launched weapon, very similar to the United States ASROC, and also similar to the Russian SS-N-15 Starfish, on which it improves. It differs from the SS-N-15 in that after launch and flight, it releases a torpedo instead of a depth charge. The missile is launched via a 66 centimetre torpedo tube, broaches the surface, and uses its solid-fuel booster to fly to the suspected location of the enemy submarine. It then jettisons the booster and the torpedo deploys a parachute, dropping into the sea and seeking its target with a pre-programmed search pattern. It has a range of 15 km at 30 knots speed. The yield of the nuclear warhead is unknown.

Torpedoes (Type 53-68 HWT/Type 65 HWT)

Nuclear-tipped torpedoes were the first Russian naval nuclear weapons, deployed in 1958. Compared to Western torpedoes, former-Soviet heavyweight torpedoes (HWT), such as those that carry nuclear warheads, are extremely conservative in design. Information on their performance capabilities is still vague, however.

CHINESE TNWS

NRDC estimates that China possesses some 150 TNWs—presumably lower yield bombs in the form of aircraft ordnance, artillery shells, atomic demolition munitions and possibly short-range missiles.[23] The deployment locations of these weapons are unknown. China also possesses about 250 "strategic" warheads, although it has only a few missiles that are able to travel intercontinental distances, and about 1,000 other missiles with ranges of up to 4,750 km. Its bomber force, normally considered part of strategic forces, has a limited reach. Transparency of Chinese nuclear forces is lacking and no official data on Chinese TNWs are available. An overview is given in Table 8. It may be

---

[23] W. M. Arkin, R. S. Norris and J. Handler, *Taking Stock—World-wide Nuclear Deployments 1998*, p. 45.

disputable which systems should be classified as "tactical" and which as "strategic" even more so as the information available is contradictory (i.e. the yield of the Julang-1 warhead).

Table 8: Chinese nuclear forces with technical properties comparable to United States and Russian TNWs (NRDC)

Category	Number	Yield	Range (km)	Warheads
Tactical weapons				
Artillery/ADMs, Short-range missiles		low kt		120
Aircraft				
Qian-5	30	5-20 kt[24]	400	
Land-based missiles				
Dong Feng-21A	36	200-300 kt	1,800	36
SLBMs				
Julang-1	12	200-300 kt, 2 Mt[25]	1,700	12

Descriptions of Chinese nuclear weapon systems with technical properties comparable to United States and Russian TNWs are compiled below:[26]

Tactical Weapons

Due to effective Chinese secrecy about its nuclear weapons programme, it is not clear whether China does indeed possess TNWs.

---

[24] Ibid.

[25] *The Military Balance 1995-6*, p. 293, as quoted by the Center for Defense Information, http://www.cdi.org/issues/nukef&f/database/chnukes.html.

[26] Ibid.

However, the general assumption is that it does. This is supported by evidence from various sources, including Chinese military exercises which assume the use of TNWs by both sides. Such weapons might consist of about 150 low-yield bombs, artillery shells, multiple-rocket system (MRS) shells, atomic demolition mines, and perhaps short-range missiles.

Qian-5

The Qian-5 is a Chinese redesign of the Soviet MiG-19 fighter. The primary visual difference is the addition of a nose cone and the addition of lateral air intakes on either side of the fuselage just forward of the swept wings. The Qian-5 is a single-seat, supersonic low level attack aircraft. It has a range of 600 km. Very little is known about Chinese atomic gravity bombs other than that they exist. The Qian-5 attack aircraft has been reported as carrying TNWs with a yield of 5-20 kilotons.

Dong Feng-21/21A IRBM

The DF-21 has a range of 1,800 km with a warhead whose yield is 200-300 kt. It is a solid-fuelled ballistic missile. It is the first truly land mobile Chinese missile, mounted on a transporter erector launcher (TEL) vehicle. The missile uses a cold launch technique whereby it is ejected from its container, with the engines igniting while airborne. Its likely targets are urban areas in Russia.

Julang 1

The Julang-1 is a medium-range SLBM capable of travelling a distance of some 2,700 km.[27]

---

[27] NRDC gives a range of 1,700 km.

BRITISH TNWs[28]

The British nuclear stockpile consists of about 160 strategic SLBM warheads and 100 WE177 tactical aircraft bombs which are being retired. The location of the tactical systems are Faslane (submarine home port, 160 warheads), RAF Marham (Tornado/WE 177, being retired, 80 warheads), Aldermaston (Laboratory), and Burghfield (warheads awaiting disassembly).

WE177A/B Gravity Bomb

The WE 177 is Britain's nuclear gravity bomb. It has a variable yield, with a minimum of 10 kilotons and a maximum of 200 kilotons for variant A, and 400 kilotons for variant B. The design lineage of the WE 177 is unclear. It seems most likely that it is a derivative of the United States B57 and B61 bombs, although other sources state it is entirely of British origin (although, with only four bomb tests in the design period between 1962 and 1965, this is unlikely). Both variants are parachute retarded for low altitude or lay down delivery (where the bomb parachutes to the ground and detonates after a preset delay in order for the aircraft to escape the blast). In 1991 Britain announced it would cut its ageing WE 177 stockpile in half, and in 1995 it announced it would eliminate it altogether by the end of 1998, which has since happened.

FRENCH TNWs[29]

France has about 400 sea-based and air-based "strategic" nuclear weapons but no systems that are officially classified as "tactical". France no longer has any nuclear gravity bombs. However, the Super Etendard,

---

[28] Weapon numbers and locations are taken from W. M. Arkin, R. S. Norris and J. Handler, *Taking Stock—World-wide Nuclear Deployments 1998*, pp. 39, 88. Their description is taken from Center for Defense Information, http://www.cdi.org/issues/nukef&f/database/uknukes.html.

[29] Descriptions of the French nuclear weapon systems are taken from Center for Defense Information,
http://www.cdi.org/issues/nukef&f/database/frnukes.html.

a carrier-based aircraft armed with a nuclear short-range attack missile (SRAM), has a range of only 850 km, and the Mirage 2000, also fitted with a nuclear SRAM has a range of 1,205 km.[30] These ranges could be classified as "tactical" according to a range-based definition. The missiles are based at Istres (20 warheads, Mirage), Luxeuil (40 warheads, Mirage), Landivisiau, Limeil-Valenton (Laboratory), and Valduc (50 warheads, assembly and disassembly). (The SLBMs are based at Ile Longue.)[31]

Super Etendard

France is the only nuclear power which still deploys, naval-based, non-SLBM nuclear weapons. These are based on two aircraft carriers which are equipped with a varying number of Super Etendard nuclear-capable strike aircraft. The Super-Etendard is a single-seat, single-engine, all-weather, fighter-bomber. It is designed for a low to medium altitude flight profile and is capable of in-flight refuelling.

Mirage 2000N

The Mirage 2000N (Nucléaire) is the nuclear-strike component of France's Force Aérienne Stratégique (FAS). It has a range of 1,205 km. The Mirage 2000N is a two-seater, single engine, delta wing, low altitude strike fighter-bomber. In mission mode, they are fitted with terrain-following radar, two inertial guidance platforms, two Magic self-defence missiles and an ECM jamming suite. They carry the ASMP short-range attack missile.

INDIA'S POSSIBLE TNWS

Possible Indian nuclear delivery systems are missiles and aeroplanes which according to their range could be classified as

---

[30] See Center for Defense Information, http://www.cdi.org/issues/nuke/f&f/database/frnukes.html. NRDC lists a range for the Super Etendard of 650 km, and for the Mirage 2000N of 2,750 km. See W. M. Arkin, R. S. Norris and J. Handler, *Taking Stock—World-wide Nuclear Deployments 1998*, p. 42.

[31] Ibid., p. 88.

"tactical". The yields of eventual Indian nuclear warheads are unknown, as is whether India is actually capable of equipping any of its delivery systems with nuclear warheads. Table 9 gives an overview of India's prospective TNW delivery systems:[32]

Table 9: Possible Indian nuclear delivery systems (CDI)

System	Number	Range (km)	Warhead Weight (kg)	Notes
Missiles				
Prithvi	100	150/250	1,000/500	May be equipped with nuclear warheads.
Agni	u.k.	2,500	1,000	May have nuclear warheads in the future.
Aircraft				
Jaguar	97	850	4,750	Could deliver nuclear bombs.
MiG-27 Flogger	148	390	4,000	Could deliver nuclear bombs.

The systems are described as follows:[33]

Prithvi

The Prithvi has a range of 150 km (army version) and 250 km (air force version). The propulsion system is based on the Soviet SA-2 surface to air missile. The missile has a distinctive appearance, with four delta-shaped wings midway down the fuselage. It is based near the border with Pakistan, on eight-wheeled Kolos Tetra trucks, which can raise the missile for launch. It uses a volatile liquid fuel launch mode, and must be

---

[32] Center for Defense Information, http://www.cdi.org/issues/nukef&f/database/nukestab.html.

[33] Center for Defense Information, http://www.cdi.org/issues/nukef&f/database/innukes.html.

fuelled immediately prior to launch. Given this significant disadvantage, a solid-fuelled version may be under development. While its circular error probable (CEP) is 250 metres, it has been reported that this could be enhanced to an unheard of 10 metres, using manoeuvrable warheads. Given the short range and planned deployment area, the target is clearly India's bitter rival, Pakistan. With its 1,000 kilogram payload, the Prithvi could clearly carry a nuclear warhead.

Agni

The Agni (which means "fire" in Indian) represents a much more ambitious project compared to the Prithvi. It is an intermediate-range missile with a range of 2,500 km. It has a curious mixture of propellents in its two stages, with the first stage using solid propellent. The second stage is liquid fuelled, using a shortened Prithvi motor system. The inertial guidance is probably an upgraded form of that used on the Prithvi. On 5 December 1996, the Indian Defence Ministry declared the Agni "technology demonstration" programme over. The missiles could be deployed given the decision to do so, however, India has yet to make this decision.

Jaguar

The Jaguar is a single seat attack aircraft with a range of 850 km. The original batch purchased from the United Kingdom was assembled in India. Subsequently the aircraft was built in India under licence. The Jaguar has an integrated attack/navigation system as well as other comparatively advanced avionic and electronic countermeasures gear. It is one of India's most capable ground attack aircraft. As such, it is one of the primary candidates to carry India's limited number of nuclear weapons.

MiG-27 Flogger M

The MiG-27 Flogger M is a single-seat attack fighter with a range of 390 km. It has variable sweep wings, and an integrated attack/navigation system. It was designed by the Soviet Union in the late 1970s. Its design was based on the MiG-23B Flogger, but had enhanced engines and avionics. Since the Russian version can carry TNWs, the possibility that the Indian MiG-27M could potentially be tasked with carrying Indian nuclear gravity bombs cannot be ruled out.

PAKISTAN'S POSSIBLE TNWS

Possible Pakistani nuclear delivery systems include missiles and aircraft which according to their range could be classified as "tactical". The yields of eventual Pakistani nuclear warheads are unknown as is whether or not Pakistan would be able to affix these to its delivery systems. Table 10 gives an overview of Pakistan's likely nuclear-weapon delivery systems:[34]

Table 10: Pakistani possible nuclear delivery systems (CDI)

System	Number	Range (km)	Warhead Weight (kg)	Notes
Missiles				
Hatf 1	18	80	500	
Hatf 2	u.k.	300	500	
M-11 (DF-11, CSS-7)	40	300	80	Supplied by China.
Aircraft				
F-16 Falcon	34	630	5,400	Gravity nuclear bomb delivery role.

The systems are described as follows:[35]

Hatf 1

The Hatf-1 (which means "deadly" in Pakistani) is a recent short-range ballistic missile produced by Pakistan which has a range of 80 km.

---

[34] Center for Defense Information, http://www.cdi.org/issues/nukef&f/database/nukestab.html.

[35] Center for Defense Information, http://www.cdi.org/issues/nukef&f/database/panukes.html.

The missile was developed with China's aid, although Pakistan maintains it was produced without outside assistance. However, both Hatf missiles resemble the Chinese M-series missiles, so China's technical aid seems likely. Little is known about the missile or its role.

Hatf-2

The Hatf-2 missile was apparently developed in tandem with the Hatf-1 in the early 1980s, possibly with Chinese aid. It has a range of 300 km. Little information is available on its deployment, and the missile is probably still in advanced development. Both stages of the Hatf-2 are believed to have solid propellent. It is reportedly a mobile system, but it is carried on converted Second World War-era anti-aircraft gun trailers instead of modern TELs.

M-11 (CSS-7)

The M-11 is the Chinese Dong Feng 11 which the Pakistanis reportedly have purchased. The M-11 has two solid-fuelled stages as well as terminal guidance, which provides increased accuracy and a range of 300 kilometres. The intelligence community has claimed that China sold over 30 missiles to Pakistan, despite denials by both Governments. The missiles are allegedly stored in crates at Pakistan's Sargodha Air Force Base.

F-16 Falcon

The F-16 Fighting Falcon has been a very successful American fighter, produced in great numbers and widely exported (see description above). The United States owes Pakistan 77 more F-16s, but refuses to deliver them.

ISRAEL'S POSSIBLE TNWS

Possible Israeli nuclear delivery systems consist of missiles and aircraft which according to their range could be classified as "tactical". The yields of Israeli nuclear warheads are unknown, though it is widely believed that Israel does possess nuclear warheads and that it is able to mount these on suitable delivery systems. Table 11 gives an overview of Israeli delivery systems.[36]

Table 11: Possible Israeli TNW delivery systems (CDI)

System	Number	Range (km)	Warhead Weight (kg)
Missiles			
Jericho 1	~50	500	500
Jericho 2	~50	1,500	1,000
Aircraft			
F-4E-2000 Phantom	50	1,600	7,200
F-16 Falcon	205	630	5,400

The systems are described as follows:[37]

Jericho 1 SRBM

The Jericho I is a short-range ballistic missile (SRBM) with a range of 500 km and is based on the French Dassault MD-600 design. The missile is reported as having a 500 kilogram high explosive warhead, but could be fitted with a nuclear warhead as well. The Jericho is carried on a wheeled TEL vehicle or on railroad car launchers. A total of approximately 100 Jericho I and II missiles are believed to have been constructed. Israel is reportedly trying to procure requisite technology to improve the accuracy of the Jericho missiles, as it currently lacks the

---

[36] Center for Defense Information, http://www.cdi.org/issues/nukef&f/database/nukestab.html.

[37] Center for Defense Information, http://www.cdi.org/issues/nukef&f/database/isnukes.html.

components necessary for the manufacture of precision gyroscopes and sensors.

Jericho-2 MRBM

The Jericho II improved greatly upon the performance of its predecessor. Unlike the single-stage Jericho I, the Jericho II has two stages, which allow for a greatly increased range of 1,500 kilometres as opposed to 500 km. Like its predecessor, the Jericho II is land mobile. In addition to inertial guidance, it may have some sort of terminal guidance as well, to increase accuracy. The payload is reportedly double that of the Jericho I (i.e. 1,000 kilograms), more than enough to carry a nuclear warhead. It is not known whether the Israelis have assigned nuclear warheads to the Jericho II, but given the great range, payload and capability of the system, this is very likely. With its long range, the Jericho II brings a dramatic increase in Israel's delivery capabilities. The missile is capable of hitting the entire panoply of targets in the Middle East (particularly Iran), as well as south-western Russia. The Jericho I and II are deployed near Kfar Zachariah and Sderot Micha in the Judean foothills.[38]

F-4E-2000 Phantom

The Phantom was originally designed as a two-seat, two-engine, long-range, all-weather attack fighter-bomber aircraft for American carriers. The Israelis have the F-4E version, which was designed as a multi-role fighter capable of air superiority, close air support and interdiction missions. This version also has an additional fuselage fuel cell for increased range, as well as the leading edge slats developed for the F-4F, which give the aircraft more manoeuvrability. Today, despite a Phantom 2000 modernization programme, these aircraft are ageing. Although the F-4E is capable of carrying nuclear bombs, this role is more likely allocated to the more modern F-16s.

---

[38] Federation of American Scientists (FAS), http://www.fas.org/nuke/hew/Israel/index.html.

F-16 Falcon

The United States F-16 fighter-bomber (see description above) has been exported to Israel in large numbers. The Israeli F-16s have been extensively modified with Israeli equipment, as well as optional United States equipment, particularly enhanced jamming and electronic countermeasures equipment. Given that the Falcon is probably the most capable Israeli attack aircraft, it is likely that it is also tasked with the eventual delivery of nuclear weapons.

Recent UNIDIR Publications

Tactical Nuclear Weapons: A Perspective from Ukraine, by A. Shevtsov, A. Yizhak, A. Gavrish and A. Chumakov, 2001, United Nations publication (forthcoming)

Bound to Cooperate: Conflict, Peace and People in Sierra Leone, by Anatole Ayissi and Robin-Edward Poulton (eds), 2000, 213p., United Nations publication, Sales No. GV.E.00.0.20.

The Small Arms Problem in Central Asia: Features and Implications, by Bobi Pirseyedi, 2000, 120p., United Nations publication, Sales No. GV.E.00.0.6.

Peacekeeping in Africa: Capabilities and Culpabilities, by Eric G. Berman and Katie E. Sams, 2000, 540p., United Nations publication, Sales No. GV.E.00.0.4.

West Africa Small Arms Moratorium: High-Level Consultations on the Modalities for the Implementation of PCASED, by Jacqueline Seck, 2000, 81p., United Nations publication, UNIDIR/2000/2
 * Existe également en français: *Moratoire ouest-africain sur les armes légères : Consultations de haut niveau sur les modalités de la mise en œuvre du PCASED*, par Jacqueline Seck, 2000, 83p., United Nations publication, UNIDIR/2000/2

The Potential Uses of Commercial Satellite Imagery in the Middle East, 1999, 58p., United Nations publication, UNIDIR/99/13

Small Arms Control: Old Weapons, New Issues, by Lora Lumpe (ed.), 1999, 302p., ISBN 0 7546 2076 X, published for UNIDIR by Ashgate Publishing Limited (Aldershot)

Fissile Material Stocks: Characteristics, Measures and Policy Options, by William Walker and Frans Berkhout, 1999, 66p., United Nations publication, Sales No. GV.E.99.0.15.

Collaboration internationale et construction de la paix en Afrique de l'Ouest : l'exemple du Mali, 1999, 64p., United Nations publication, UNIDIR/99/4

The Implications of South Asia's Nuclear Tests for the Non-Proliferation and Disarmament Regimes, 1999, 28p., United Nations publication, UNIDIR/99/2

Sensors for Peace: Applications, Systems and Legal Requirements for Monitoring in Peace Operations, by Jürgen Altmann, Horst Fisher and Henny J. van der Graaf (eds), 1998, 298p., United Nations publication, Sales No. GV.E.98.0.28.

Non-Offensive Defense in the Middle East, by Bjørn Møller, Gustav Däniker, Shmuel Limone and Ioannis A. Stivachtis, 1998, 150p., United Nations publication, Sales No. GV.E.98.0.27.

Curbing Illicit Trafficking in Small Arms and Sensitive Technologies: An Action-Oriented Agenda, by Péricles Gasparini Alves and Daiana Cipollone (eds), 1998, 286p., United Nations publication, Sales No. GV.E.98.0.8.

* Also available in Spanish: *Represión del tráfico ilícito de armas pequeñas y tecnologías sensibles: Una agenda orientada hacia la acción*, por Péricles Gasparini Alves y Daiana Cipollone (eds), 1998, 288p., United Nations publication, Sales No. GV.S.98.0.8.

Disarmament and Conflict Resolution Project - Managing Arms in Peace Processes: Training, by Ilkka Tiihonen, Virginia Gamba, Jakkie Potgieter, Barbara Carrai, Claudia Querner and Steve Tulliu, 1998, 170p., United Nations publication, Sales No. GV.E.98.0.6.

A Peace of Timbuktu—Democratic Governance, Development and African Peacemaking, by Robin-Edward Poulton and Ibrahim ag Youssouf, 1998, 388p., United Nations publication, Sales No. GV.E.98.0.3.

* Existe également en français: *La paix de Tombouctou—Gestion démocratique, développement et construction africaine de la paix*, par Robin-Edward Poulton et Ibrahim ag Youssouf, 1998, 437p., United Nations publication, Sales No. GV.F.98.0.3.

Increasing Access to Information Technology for International Security: Forging Co-operation Among Research Institutes, by Péricles Gasparini Alves (ed.), 1997, 242p., United Nations publication, Sales No. GV.E.97.0.23.

Operación CEIBO: Ejercicio Combinado de Operaciones de Mantenimiento de la Paz entre Uruguay y Argentina, editado por Cnel. Carlos Pagola y Cnel. Jorge Tereso, 1997, 63p., United Nations publication, Sales No. GV.S.97.0.30.

Nuclear-Weapon-Free Zones in the 21st Century, by Péricles Gasparini Alves and Daiana Cipollone (eds), 1997, 169p., United Nations publication, Sales No. GV.E.97.0.29.

* Also available in Spanish: *Las Zonas Libres de Armas Nucleares en el Siglo XXI*, editado por Péricles Gasparini Alves y Daiana Cipollone, 1997, 180p., United Nations publication, Sales No. GV.S.97.0.29.

The Transfer of Sensitive Technologies and the Future of Control Regimes, by Péricles Gasparini Alves and Kerstin Hoffman (eds), 1997, 150p., United Nations publication, Sales No. GV.E.97.0.10.

Disarmament and Conflict Resolution Project - Managing Arms in Peace Processes: Nicaragua and El Salvador, by Paulo Wrobel, 1996, 250p., United Nations publication, Sales No. GV.E.97.0.1.

Disarmament and Conflict Resolution Project - Managing Arms in Peace Processes: Haiti, by Marcos Mendiburu and Sarah Meek, 1996, 97p., United Nations publication, Sales No. GV.E.96.0.34.

Disarmament and Conflict Resolution Project - Managing Arms in Peace Processes: The Issues, by Estanislao Angel Zawels, Stephen John Stedman, Donald C.F. Daniel, David Cox, Jane Boulden, Fred Tanner, Jakkie Potgieter and Virginia Gamba, 1996, 234p., United Nations publication, Sales No. GV.E.96.0.33.

Disarmament and Conflict Resolution Project - Managing Arms in Peace Processes: Liberia, by Clement Adibe, 1996, 129p., United Nations publication, Sales No. GV.E.96.0.23.

Disarmament and Conflict Resolution Project - Managing Arms in Peace Processes: Aspects of Psychological Operations and Intelligence, by Andrei Raevsky, 1996, 46p., United Nations publication, Sales No. GV.E.96.0.21.

Evolving Trends in the Dual Use of Satellites, by Péricles Gasparini Alves (ed.), 1996, 180p., United Nations publication, Sales No. GV.E.96.0.20.

A Zone Free of Weapons of Mass Destruction in the Middle East, by Jan Prawitz and James F. Leonard, 1996, 134p., United Nations publication, Sales No. GV.E.96.0.19.

Disarmament and Conflict Resolution Project - Managing Arms in Peace Processes: Mozambique, by Eric Berman, 1996, 103p., United Nations publication, Sales No. GV.E.96.0.18.

Disarmament and Conflict Resolution Project - Small Arms Management and Peacekeeping in Southern Africa, by Christopher Smith, Peter Batchelor and Jakkie Potgieter, 1996, 125p., United Nations publication, Sales No. GV.E.96.0.16.

Disarmament and Conflict Resolution Project - Managing Arms in Peace Processes: Cambodia, by Jianwei Wang, 1996, 243p., United Nations publication, Sales No. GV.E.96.0.14.

Disarmament and Conflict Resolution Project - Managing Arms in Peace Processes: Croatia and Bosnia-Herzegovina, by Barbara

Ekwall-Uebelhart and Andrei Raevsky, 1996, 411p., United Nations publication, Sales No. GV.E.96.0.6.

Disarmament Forum / *Forum du désarmement* (quarterly / trimestriel)

four•2000	Biological Weapons: From the BWC to Biotech
quatre•2000	Les armes biologiques: de la Convention aux biotechnologies
three•2000	Peacekeeping: evolution or extinction?
trois•2000	Maintien de la paix: évolution ou extinction?
two•2000	Small Arms Control: the need for coordination
deux•2000	Maîtrise des armes légères: quelle coordination?
one•2000	What Next for the NPT?
un•2000	Où va le TNP?
four•1999	Framework for a Mine-free World
quatre•1999	Vers un monde sans mines
three•1999	On-site Inspections: Common Problems, Different Solutions
trois•1999	Les inspections sur place : mêmes problèmes, autres solutions
two•1999	Fissile Materials: Scope, Stocks and Verification
deux•1999	Un traité sur les matières fissiles: portée, stocks et vérification
one•1999	The New Security Debate
un•1999	Le nouveau débat sur la sécurité

كيفية الحصول على منشورات الأمم المتحدة

يمكن الحصول على منشورات الأمم المتحدة من المكتبات ودور التوزيع في جميع أنحاء العالم. استعلم عنها من المكتبة التي تتعامل معها أو اكتب إلى: الأمم المتحدة، قسم البيع في نيويورك أو في جنيف.

如何购取联合国出版物

联合国出版物在全世界各地的书店和经售处均有发售。请向书店询问或写信到纽约或日内瓦的联合国销售组。

HOW TO OBTAIN UNITED NATIONS PUBLICATIONS

United Nations publications may be obtained from bookstores and distributors throughout the world. Consult your bookstore or write to: United Nations, Sales Section, New York or Geneva.

COMMENT SE PROCURER LES PUBLICATIONS DES NATIONS UNIES

Les publications des Nations Unies sont en vente dans les librairies et les agences dépositaires du monde entier. Informez-vous auprès de votre libraire ou adressez-vous à : Nations Unies, Section des ventes, New York ou Genève.

КАК ПОЛУЧИТЬ ИЗДАНИЯ ОРГАНИЗАЦИИ ОБЪЕДИНЕННЫХ НАЦИЙ

Издания Организации Объединенных Наций можно купить в книжных магазинах и агентствах во всех районах мира. Наводите справки об изданиях в вашем книжном магазине или пишите по адресу: Организация Объединенных Наций, Секция по продаже изданий, Нью-Йорк или Женева.

COMO CONSEGUIR PUBLICACIONES DE LAS NACIONES UNIDAS

Las publicaciones de las Naciones Unidas están en venta en librerías y casas distribuidoras en todas partes del mundo. Consulte a su librero o diríjase a: Naciones Unidas, Sección de Ventas, Nueva York o Ginebra.

Printed at United Nations, Geneva
GE.00-03944–December 2000–1,825

UNIDIR/2000/20

United Nations publication
Sales No. GV.E.00.0.21

ISBN 92-9045-136-X